CREATIVE ENTREPRENEURSHIP

THE WALT DISNEY WAY

Virender Kapoor is a thinker, an educationist and an inspirational guru. An alumnus of IIT Bombay and the former director of a prestigious management institute under the Symbiosis umbrella, he also holds a master's in International Relations and Strategic Studies from Pune University. His books on emotional intelligence, leadership and self-help have been translated into several regional and foreign languages. A prolific writer, he regularly contributes to *The Times of India, The Economic Times, Rediff.com* and several management magazines. To know more about him, log on to www.virenderkapoor.com or mail him at virenderkapoor21@yahoo.com

Also by the author:

Speaking: The Modi Way

Leadership: The Gandhi Way

Innovation: The Einstein Way

Excellence: The Amitabh Bachchan Way

Winning: The Chanakya Way

Resilience: The Hawking Way

Succeeding: The Akshay Kumar Way

CREATIVE ENTREPRENEURSHIP

THE WALT DISNEY WAY

VIRENDER KAPOOR

RUPA

Published by
Rupa Publications India Pvt. Ltd 2022
7/16, Ansari Road, Daryaganj
New Delhi 110002

Sales centres:
Allahabad Bengaluru Chennai
Hyderabad Jaipur Kathmandu
Kolkata Mumbai

ISBN: 978-93-5520-236-9

First impression 2022

10 9 8 7 6 5 4 3 2 1

Printed at HT Media Ltd, Greater Noida

Contents

Contents

1

Sketch of a Cartoonist

'I don't like formal gardens. I like wild nature. It's just the wilderness instinct in me, I guess.'

—Walter Elias Disney

Everyone knows Walt Disney, but do they know Walt Disney? I would argue that most of us don't. At least that was my impression when I started researching about this larger-than-life icon, who has left behind a legacy in the domain of creativity that no one in the field has been able to surpass.

By the time he died in 1966, at the age of 65, Walter Elias Disney had created such impactful and monumental characters that they would probably live on for another century. He created a separate mammoth stream of entertainment, which I would like to call 'cartoonistology' and an ism of sorts that people could have never even imagined had he not created it.

He was born with an incredible talent to imagine

characters, plots, stories and turn them into engaging narratives. What kept his eye on the ball till his very last day was his commitment to his work and his passion for creating the best in the field of animation.

What made him create such outstanding characters? It was his unparalleled dedication. It was as if he lived in a world of his own world—a world full of cartoons, characters and stories. He was so obsessed with Mickey Mouse after he created it that his wife called herself a 'mouse widow'! Eccentric as he was, as far as his creative competence was concerned, he would disagree with the best artists of his time and would take huge risks in doing what he wanted. He was a workaholic, a creative maniac who constantly pushed the envelope and kept raising the bar—often competing with himself. Every work done by his huge team of professional artists in Walt Disney Studios had to be approved by him. He kept a tight control on creativity and refused delegating authority to his team. A nod of appreciation from Walter could catapult the morale of the best of artists to seventh heaven. He would look at his own creation and ask, 'Could we have done it any better?'

He had created a concept of a 'sweat box', which is equivalent to watching rushes in mainstream cinema today. Walter would view the rough animation scenes created by his artists and animators in a cramped room, nicknamed the sweat box, where he would critique and assess their work. The animators sitting in the room would often sweat in anticipation, worrying about how he would react to their work.

Working for Passion and Perfection, Not Money

Walter was never after money. He poured whatever he earned into his next project and always said that money is a by-product of great work. Therefore, he was always in debt for his studio! He lived a simple life and only allowed himself small luxuries, like travelling first-class when he could afford. He was neither good at managing money, nor at being organized; he even despised the word 'organization' when it came to creativity. He wanted an absolutely relaxed and an informal atmosphere at the workplace to draw the best out of people. According to his employees, he had an uncanny way of getting the best out of every artist. In the world of cinema, too, where actors perform, a good film director is the one who is able to get the best out of his cast.

Walter was always ahead of his times and was tech savvy, wisely adapting to it quickly to integrate and augment his creative work. Being the pioneer in his field, his ambition was to become the most revered and the greatest animator in the world.

Walter was the one who brought sound effect into cartoon films and later integrated music, which would infuse life into motion pictures. He devised methods to synchronize music with the movement of his cartoon characters and was also quick to understand the impact of colour in cinema. This was specifically true for animation, where a coloured Donald Duck or a Mickey Mouse looked several times better than a drab black-and-white one. Here, too, he took a risk because Technicolor was just launched and was prohibitively expensive, much more than the regular black-and-white films. Yet he put all that he had into producing coloured cartoons.

He was lucky to have a brother who managed his financial affairs, day-to-day operations and raised funds for Disney projects. Roy Oliver Disney was Walter's strongest pillar of support, and despite being an elder brother—by eight years—he was prepared to work under his shadow. Mature and accommodating, he was honest and loyal to his younger brother. And Roy, no doubt, was the one major reason why Walter could achieve what he set his eyes on, in his huge career. Roy knew that Walter was an extraordinary person who was meant to create something unparalleled and thus stood by his side—this was a rare bond between brothers, based on trust, honesty and integrity.

Though Roy disagreed with Walter on many occasions and was tight-fisted with finances, he was accommodating when it came to creativity and spending money on a project Walter had set his mind on. Walter would, more often than not, overshoot his budget and ask Roy to get more funds, which the latter always managed to. It was a balancing act between the two brothers.

Not an Instant Success

We tend to think that Walter, with his ability to create well-loved cartoons, was an instant success and made a lot of money. However, it was not quite so. He had to struggle for most of his professional career to make a mark in the field of entertainment, despite being one of the most imaginative cartoonist of his times. His journey was never a cakewalk and, in fact, was far from it. He lived in abject poverty during the first decade of his career, and it was only when Mickey Mouse made its first appearance in 1928, when Walter was 27 years old, that things started going well for him. He was always trying to outdo himself, and, in his quest, he was always short of money to produce better cartoon films. It should be noted that in Hollywood there is a 'dog eat dog' kind of vulturous culture that has existed right from the beginning of the cinema industry, and Walter had to survive it all. Film and entertainment industry was and still is merciless and ruthless when it comes to failures—there is no room for failures. You are catapulted skywards if you succeed, but in case you fail, you can as easily be dumped.

He created umpteen characters, some of which became legends—Mickey Mouse, Donald Duck, The Three Little Pigs, Bambi, Snow White and the Seven Dwarfs. These characters had human-like qualities, with which young and old could relate alike.

In 1919, Walter took up a job with a commercial

artist at Pesmen-Rubin Commercial Art Studio. There, he drew commercial illustrations for advertising and theatre. He also befriended fellow artist Ubbe Ert Iwwerks later, with whom he would have a long-term association throughout his career. After the art studio's revenues declined, the two got fired and started their own small enterprise. This also didn't work out and hence they joined Kansas City Film Ad Company, run by one Mr A.V. Cauger and learnt to make animation with cut-out technique. This marked the starting point of Walter's career in the animation industry.

He wanted to work on animations through cel technique, Cauger was not up for it. Therefore, Walter, with a friend Fred Harman, opened a small company. Their main client was Newman Theatre and the short cartoons they produced for them were sold as 'Newman's Laugh-O-Grams'. He then tried his hand at making his first 12-minute one-reel animation film called *Alice in Wonderland*. This also didn't pick up many returns, but it paved the way for Walter.

Tryst with Destiny: Hollywood

Walter moved to Hollywood in July 1923. Although New York was the centre of the cartoon industry, he wanted to go to Los Angeles, where he hoped to become a live-action film director; he also wanted to be close to his brother Roy, who was convalescing after contracting tuberculosis there.

He had started his career in creative field by making cartoons for commercial art and making slides for theatres. He got interested in animation and, with borrowed books and a camera, started learning and experimenting at home.

Walter was so immersed in his work that he never had the time to court women. He got married to Lillian Bounds in 1925, who he had hired as an ink artist for his own small establishment. She did not have much interest in Hollywood's social circle and was simply happy in supporting her husband, being a good wife and a dedicated mother to their two daughters.

Walter created a large number of characters throughout his career at a frantic pace, one after the other. After the success of Mickey Mouse, he produced *The Three Little Pigs* in 1933. Media lapped it up and praised it as the 'most successful short animation of all time', and it led to a further expansion of his studio staff to 200 people. By now, Walter had understood the power of telling emotionally gripping stories through the medium of animation, which interested the audience. He was the first one to create a story department, the work of which was separate from what artists and animators did. The storyboard people were responsible for detailing the plots and stories of Disney films.

Other Contributions of Walt Disney

Walter's creativity only proliferated. After being

successful as an animator and creating short cartoon films, he started working on creating full-length feature films. He produced more than 100 films, and the first one was *Snow White and the Seven Dwarfs,* which was premiered in Los Angeles in 1937 and grossed $1.5 million—an unheard amount those days. It won him eight Oscars.

Walt Disney Studios became one of the largest and the most successful movie production houses in the world. Some of his most important and famous films were *Pinocchio* (1940), *Fantasia* (1940), *Dumbo* (1941), *Bambi* (1942), *Cinderella* (1950), *Treasure Island* (1950), *Alice in Wonderland* (1951), *Peter Pan* (1953), *Lady and the Tramp* (1955), *Sleeping Beauty* (1959) and *101 Dalmatians* (1961).

The narratives of Walter's movies were such that they were a treat to watch for both children and adults. It had an international appeal and was not restricted to the United States alone. Each one of them was a creative classic that one could watch several times and yet not get bored.

He was also among the first people to use television as an entertainment medium. The *Zorro* and *Davy Crockett* series were extremely popular with children. The *Mickey Mouse Club,* a variety show featuring a cast of teenagers known as the Mouseketeers, was a big hit. Walter used his Sunday night TV show, *The Wonderful World of Color,* to promote his theme parks.

Walter came up with the idea of creating a theme

park where children and families could enjoy fun-filled rides and also meet Disney characters. The first Disneyland went live in 1955, when he was 54 years old. It was built on an orange grove and spread across 160-acre land.[1] It was a historical landmark. In a short time, the investment into this park went tenfold. It became a 'must visit' tourist attraction for people from across the world. One has to credit Walter for his creative imagination and the scale at which he thought and acted. Imagine a person struggling for a few dollars at the age of 30 who then goes on to invest millions in a new unchartered business within a couple of decades!

America became America because Americans always imagined big and did things on a colossal scale. If they built highways, they were broad and huge; their buildings were skyscrapers (as if scraping the sky); and they built tanks, submarines, ships and aircraft in huge numbers. They built the biggest aircraft carriers, luxury ships, transport and commercial aircraft.

People like Walter and many such Americans built on this spirit, imagining and creating larger-than-life things, and that is what America stands for. Such thinking and spirit is what makes America a superpower today.

---

[1]Taylor, Alan. 'Opening Day at Disneyland: Photos From 1955', *The Atlantic*, 24 July 2019, https://bit.ly/3q3rMyy. Accessed on 14 March 2022.

Awards Were Plenty

Relentlessly working towards perfection and impactful entertainment, Walter went all guns blazing after the creation of Mickey Mouse. He won his first competitive Academy Award for Best Short Subject (cartoon category) for the film *Flowers and Trees;* he received his first Honorary Academy Award in 1932 at the age of 31 for the creation of Mickey Mouse.

The cinema and film fraternity bestowed on him a huge number of awards, which probably no other person has been able to surpass. In his career spanning a little more than four decades, he received 26 Academy awards, three Golden Globe awards and one Emmy.

> *'When you believe in a thing, believe in it all the way, implicitly and unquestionable.'*
>
> —Walter Elias Disney

2

Rough, Yet a Happy Childhood

'Passion is energy. Feel the power that comes from focusing on what excites you.'

—Oprah Winfrey

Walter Elias Disney was born to Elias and Flora Disney on 5 December 1901 in Chicago, America. Elias, his father who worked for a while as a carpenter, lived under the shadow of his younger brother, Robert Disney who had acquired some wealth speculating in real estate, oil and, to some extent, in gold mines too. Elias worked as a contractual employee to build homes, and his wife Flora helped him earn and add to whatever little they could manage. Frugal as he was, with Robert's contacts and help, he managed to invest a little in real estate out of the money he had earned as a carpenter building a few homes for the workers in his area.

Facing financial troubles, both Elias and Flora

leaned more towards faith rather than depending only on their hard work. Elias, by now, was in his 40s and had started participating in the activities of church very enthusiastically. During these difficult times, Walter was born.

Troubles never spared Elias—eventually, the area in Chicago where they lived became unsafe owing to rise in crime. He started looking for a safer town and decided to shift his family to Marceline, Missouri, where his brother had bought a farm for himself.

He Loved Nature and Drawing

Elias bought a 40-acre land a mile away from the 500-acre farm owned by his brother, Robert. Though Walter did not spend very many years on the farm, he could remember each and every detail of those days, as his wife went on to recount years down the line. Walter, perhaps, loved nature, with all the apple trees and animals it had to offer—the farm life left a deep impression on him. It was a heaven for city lads who went on to experience the pleasure of being surrounded by all sorts of animals like rabbits, squirrels, pigs, foxes and raccoons. These were his best days as he recalled later while talking to his family on several occasions. He had a close affinity with nature and animals, which perhaps prompted and helped him draw animal cartoons in his later years. Those were his halcyon days—carefree and full of fun.

It was here that his aunt Margaret, Robert's wife, got the kids some gifts, which included a couple of pencils and a drawing board. It was then that he realized that he loved drawing and was encouraged by his aunt who acknowledged that he was talented. Walter had another encounter with his artistic side when he used the the tar loaded in drums at his farm to draw designs on the outside walls of their home using a stick. The wall became a memorial of his art, which was left behind when they moved away from the farm.

Meanwhile, there came an understanding that his father, Elias, was not cut out for farming and, in fact, disdained it. Money was always the problem, and it was difficult for the family to lead a decent life. Farming, in any case, was not a rewarding business.

Elias was left frail and weak after he turned sick. The family had to sell their stock, their land and tools and move to a nearby town, Kansas City. Yet Walter remembered every detail of his farm life till the very end, and it helped him recreate the animals and his carefree days among woods and trees while working on his movies.

Living in the city was a disappointment, as the house they now lived in was very small and cramped. In the first decade of the twentieth century, population in the town had doubled, and it brought with it problems of law and order, and scarcity of goods necessary for decent living. Ruth, Walter's younger sister, used to accompany him to a nearby amusement park. They were barred from entering, as they could not afford to buy tickets, and ended up watching the rides only from outside. This may have served as a motivation for him to come up with Disneyland, which was materialized in his later days.

Struggle for Survival

To earn decent money, his father bought a paper route for the local newspaper, *Kansas City Star,* which would give him a steady income. Paper distribution became the central point of their very existence and their livelihood relied on this circuit of delivering morning and evening newspapers. The three of them—Walter, Roy and Elias—would fill up the carts as early as 3.30 a.m. and take them to distribution points. Walter, who was just nine at the time, had to get up every day when it was still dark, work on distributing the papers for several hours and then attend school. In the evening, the three would deliver the evening paper.

On Saturdays, he collected the fees, and on Sundays, he had a double load! As a result, Walter slept in his class almost every other day. As any child, he enjoyed being on the streets initially. He liked his job at first but soon started getting sick of the routine. Roy stopped delivering newspapers once he got a job at a bank as a clerk. Their father now made Walter work during the recess hour of his school to sell candies for earning a little more. As a result, Walter had no time at all to play. He carried on with the routine relentlessly for six years, missing only five weeks in between, when he came down with a severe cold. The kind of lifestyle he led as a child took a toll on him—even 40 years later, he would sometimes wake up in the middle of the night, drenched in sweat as a result of nightmares, wherein he dreamt he had missed some customer on the route and had forgotten to deliver the newspaper.

During the course of his difficult childhood, the only positive thing Walter learnt was the value of free time and the spurts when he could have some fun. Even after all this hard work, the family was still short of money, and he was asked to deliver theatre bills and ice creams in summers. His childhood was one long ordeal interspersed with simple thrills like getting a new pair of shoes for Christmas.

Walter's father himself was frugal, and the children never saw him enjoy any luxury. Elias was honest, disciplined and had a strong moral code of conduct. He practised fiscal stringency, learning to stay within his means, and taught the same to his children. He also had a volcanic temper and would not spare the rod whenever he found his children not falling in line. He was a serious man, and as if in rebellion, Walter turned out to be his opposite—he was blithe despite all the hardships. He was an antithesis to Elias. As a result, Walter was always found joking and often pulling pranks on his father.

Thinking his son should become a musician,

Elias got him enrolled in music classes, hoping he would learn how to play a violin—one of the most difficult instruments to play. Walter claimed that he had no musical inclination and didn't really have an ear for music, which was a prerequisite to become a professional. In a few months' time, he stopped attending the music classes.

Later in his life, Walter complained that he wished his family was a little more relaxed and fun-loving. But, he found the environment of the Disney household too solemn and serious. In fact, he once mentioned, 'There was nothing unhappy in the family, but the problem was they were just not used to having fun.' Luckily, he found happiness in the neighbouring family of Pfeiffers, who almost adopted him. It became Walter's second home and acted as an escape from his own, where he could not find a creative and joyful atmosphere, which was imperative for a child like him.

Finding Thrill in Small Things

Walter's school friend, Walt Pfeiffer, also loved acting and pulling pranks as he did. Walter considered the Pfeiffer home as his 'laughing place'. The two boys would put on acts in vaudeville theaters and call it the 'The Two Walts'.[2]

---

[2]'Pfeiffer, Walt', D23: The Official Disney Fan Club, https://bit.ly/3L22zN6. Accessed on 14 March 2022.

Walter, being an attention-seeker, would do anything in school to catch the attention of his friends. He staged short plays and took part in fancy dress competitions. He gradually started taking stage acting seriously and started imagining himself as an actor of sorts. He did finally get into show business later in his life, but that was of course in a different genre altogether.

Walter never stopped drawing. In his school, he would make drawings on the sides of his notebooks and entertain his friends by riffling those—an act of animation in the making! He would never let go of a chance where he could draw. He would decorate glass windows and stone walls in the town with pictures and cartoons. While his friends played basketball or other outdoor games, he would draw, even though drawing in those days was considered an effeminate hobby and deemed as being sissy. He was almost always immersed in his imaginative world, and his friends recalled that he was always considered a 'dreamer'. His teacher, Daisy Beck, encouraged him to draw. A classmate later recalled that everyone at school felt that he would go on to become a genius and a creator.

Walter realized his works were being appreciated, especially when a barber gave him a free hair cut for his cartoons, which he displayed in his shop. This encouraged him to continue drawing every day. He watched cartoonists in newspaper offices drawing cartoons and admired them. He got his first pay—seven dollars—from his school principal for a comic character that he had drawn.

An Artistic Journey Begins

Though his father could not fathom the passion that his son had for drawing, he allowed him to attend classes once a week at the Kansas City Art Institute located at YMCA. Walter had two options in his mind—either to become a stage performer through acting or pursue drawing and become a cartoonist. As he got more accolades for his talent, he began harbouring dreams of becoming a cartoonist for a newspaper, as at that time that was the only occupation available for someone with talents such as his. When his father shifted to Chicago, Walter joined William McKinley High School. He was recognized as a very good artist within just a few months and was selected as a cartoonist for the school magazine, *The McKinley Voice*. He was given time off classes to draw cartoons, and this put him on a fast road to displaying his talent.

By now, First World War had started, and his brother Roy had joined the navy. Walter started making cartoons that centered around the war and dabbled in a bit of political satire as well. Such was his love and passion for the art that when he was not drawing, he was simply thinking about it. He hoped to get a job someday as a cartoonist at one of the leading newspapers.

Walter's father was convinced by Carey Orr, a reputed cartoonist in those days, that his son must attend some of the formal classes that he conducted at the Chicago Academy of Fine Arts. Here, Walter was exposed to drawing live models for the first time, and he was so into it that he would not even take a toilet break! Here, he also realized that fine arts was not his cup of tea and his inclination was more towards drawing caricatures. Taking classes on cartooning, conducted by Leroy Gossett who worked at the *Chicago Herald*, was what he called a turning point in his career. Here, he found his real love—cartooning.

> *'I had a very happy childhood, but I wasn't that happy a child. I liked being alone and creating characters and voices. I think that's when your creativity is developed, when you're young. I liked the world of the imagination because it was an easy place to go to.'*
>
> —David Walliams

3

Early Encounters with Art, Passion and Survival

'You may not realize it when it happens, but a kick in the teeth may be the best thing in the world for you.'

—Walter Eias Disney

Having identified pretty early his passion for cartooning and caricature, Walter was not sure how this talent would proliferate into a viable profession. Landing a job at a newspaper as a cartoonist was still a distant dream. Therefore, he did not abandon the idea of show business—acting and performing arts. He tried his hand at magic and showing tricks on the stage in front of a small audience. His idea was to do something that he felt he had some talent for and, most of all, enjoyed working at. His shows were not appreciated, and as an alternative, he tried his hand at photography. However, even that didn't give him much success.

Very few of us realize our true calling at a young age and even fewer actually make the necessary effort to follow through their passion. Therefore, a lot of talent just goes to waste. Many a times, our parents discourage us from following our passion and instead make us pursue what they feel is right for us. Walter may have been lucky that his parents, especially his father who was the decision-maker of the family, didn't have the time or money to give him any worthwhile direction or a professional choice to make. Hence, he was left to fend for himself, which was a blessing in disguise, as he kept his focus on his talent without any parental interference.

Walter was always a shy person as far as girls were concerned. Yet girls liked him for his looks and for his creative work, which was hard to come across and unusual in those days. His girlfriend, Beatrice Conover, was the editor of their school magazine. She believed that Walter would do very well in life and become famous one day.

Since he was not getting a foothold in cartooning, which was his first love, he took a job in a factory, where he made boxes, crushed apples and did all sorts of odd jobs, sometimes working even as a nightwatchman. Yet he drew whenever he would get some free time at hand. The wife of the owner of the factory appreciated his art and even bought some of his drawings. As a job offering, she asked him to make posters for a picnic she was organizing for the staff. She appreciated his work, but perhaps could never have imagined that he would become a master of his craft in a couple of decades.

If you have the gift of art in your blood, nothing can stop you. The only person that can stop you is you yourself.

> *'Follow your own passion—not your parents', not your teachers'—yours.'*
>
> —Robert Ballard

If Art is in Your Blood

Here, let me share two instances for us to draw some inspiration from.

M.F. Husain, the Indian painter and artist, also started small. He started with painting posters for Hindi films in his early days to make a living, before becoming famous for his works of modern art. An oil painting by the late Indian painter titled 'Voices' sold for a record ₹18.47 crore, the highest price for the artist's work in an auction so far.[3] He was a special invitee, along with Pablo Picasso, at the São Paulo Biennial, Brazil, in 1971.[4]

---

[3]Joshi, Sonam. 'M F Husain painting sets new record at Rs 18.5 crore', *The Times of India,* 1 September 2020, https://bit.ly/3JbNiss. Accessed on 14 March 2022.

[4]PTI, 'MF Husain: An artist who courted both fame & controversy', *The Economic Times,* 10 June 2011, https://bit.ly/3ialBEg. Accessed on 14 March 2022.

The second instance would be my first-hand experience of seeing a great artist in the making—as a child, I had seen Ranjan Sen, my neighbour in Delhi, learning how to paint from his dad Abani Sen. He was known early on as a child prodigy, and his first one-person show was attended by Jawaharlal Nehru and M.F. Husain. He could make sculptures, create fantastic figures out of scrap and, of course, spectacularly paint on canvas and paper. He got several gold medals in the Shankar International Children's Competition and won a scholarship from the Government of India. Later, he earned a Commonwealth scholarship to go to Canada and pursue formal education in fine arts. His passion for creativity is what one can see in his works displayed in top art galleries and even in private collections.

The thing about talent and art is that they flow naturally and are so strong that nothing can ever stop them, they always find a way.

Walter did various odd jobs to stay employed and also worked on his artistic skills. Unfortunately, in those days, there were little opportunities or platforms to showcase one's talent. But the man was full of pranks. When he was denied a job at the post office because of looking too young, he went back home, replaced his cap with a hat, donned a moustache, came back for the interview and got the job. With the money he saved from his earnings at the post office, he bought a movie camera and wanted to make children's films, but had to abandon this idea, as it did not make much commercial sense.

'It's not knowing what to do, it's doing what you know.'

—Tony Robbins

Willingness to Serve the Nation

Walter was keen to join the army, as, in 1918, Germans were invading Europe and both his brothers had donned the uniform by then—Roy in the navy and Ray in the army. He, too, wanted to wear the uniform and serve his country. Even before starting work at the post office, he had tried to join the navy, but was rejected, as he was underage. He applied for the Red Cross Ambulance Corps, where he found out that the minimum age requirement was 17. He was still 16 and had to get his certificate of age signed by his parents. His father refused to sign it, but Walter could persuade his mother to sign the fudged certificate showing him to be 17.

He enlisted with enthusiasm and looked at it as an opportunity of adventure and not war. He was trained hurriedly, and within a month, learnt how to drive and repair ambulances with a bit of elementary military training; his lot was packed off to France into the thick of the war. Since Walter fell sick with influenza, he remained in the training camp, while others left for France. He was devastated.

During this time, the Armistice was signed, ending the war, and now there was no chance for him to go join in the war effort. Yet as luck would have it, 50 of those enlisted were sent to France to help in the occupation process after the war, and Walter was one of them. It was an escape for him and yet an adventure of a different kind. The artist in him was still alive, and when he was not driving the ambulance or was free from his duties, he would draw sketches to decorate the mess menu and posters to advertise for hot bath for the tired troops returning from the battle front on the flaps of the ambulances. He charged a little fee to make caricatures for the soldiers, which they could send back home to their girlfriends or parents. He would make cartoons showing their troops kicking off the Germans and painted these on the walls of ambulances. He said that he found the inside and outside of the ambulance walls as good a place to draw as any. He submitted his cartoons to be published in a popular magazine but was rejected. He persevered and made caricatures on the jackets of the soldiers, charging them some money.

When he returned home, he had managed to save money from his salary earned during his days with the Red Cross. His father wanted him to join a factory and did not want him to go looking for a job as an artist in some newspaper; Walter felt that his father never understood him and his talent. By now he had matured, grown physically and was ready to face the challenges ahead. His exposure with the Red Cross was something that transformed him, and he always said that it served as a lifetime experience.

Search for a Career in Art and Craft

Ready to step into the real world where he could earn a regular income, Walter needed a job.

By the end of the First World War, America had become an unrivalled and unchallenged superpower, and the mood of the nation was upbeat. The economy boomed and things looked rosy. Walter was now back in America and headed for Kansas in 1919, determined and enthusiastic of making a mark; however, he was not sure what that mark was going to be for. He knew that he wanted to do something in the creative field but was uncertain about the direction he was supposed to take.

Walter slowly grew confident about his artistic streak. Though he had no plan, he knew he would accomplish something somewhere because the zeal in him made him a go-getter. He thought from his heart and not his head. He craved to work in a good newspaper and that is all he wanted at that point. As if by chance, he saw an advertisement in *The Star* about a vacancy for an office boy, and he applied. He looked too old in his Red Cross uniform—which he wore to impress them—and as a result, he was not taken on board.

His brother Roy came to his rescue and suggested that he go and meet two of his friends who ran a commercial art shop and were looking for a hand. Walter was hired immediately, as his portfolio was impressive. Seeing his dedication and his craft, he was offered $50 a month just after a week of working there. He first rushed to his aunt who had once given him coloured pencils to draw, for which he owed her a big thank you. He yelled, 'Look they are paying me for my drawings!'

At barely 17, he was a professional artist! He learnt his craft with his two young bosses. Though not very creative work, he got the taste of creating art and selling it and finally gained a foothold in his area of interest. However, by the time Christmas was over, he lost his job and was asked to leave, as there was little work to be done.

Now, he was pushed into a corner and could not wait to get a job at a newspaper as a cartoonist. He thought of starting something of his own but had very little money. By chance, a colleague from his last job was also fired, and he came and met Walter. Ubbe Iwwerks was shy and not too ambitious. Their temperaments were poles apart, but he was a good enough guy to work with. He had no money and was desperate to get work and so Walter took their paintings and started hunting for clients in the commercial art space.

While Ubbe saw work as work, Walter was totally immersed in his job and was obsessed with it. The one common thing between them was that both were school dropouts. And, of course, both were broke and desperately looking for jobs.

Walter was an effervescent person and could multitask by painting as well as speaking to the clients. He was a powerhouse of energy. Ubbe was very meticulous, focused on his work and was effortless with the brush and board. It was a good combination. They started Iwwerks-Disney and worked in all earnestness. They managed to get hold of some office space through the owner of a magazine.

Ubbe was penniless and, therefore, Walter had to use his savings earned from his Red Cross days to buy equipment. The duo was a little skeptical about the viability of their venture. Ubbe asked Walter to take up a job with Kansas City Slide Company, which was offering $35 a week, for this would give the duo a steady income, while Ubbe held fort at their small enterprise.

Walter was hired by Mr A.V. Cauger who had employed 20 employees by then and was doing good business, earning almost a million dollars a year. They were into making promotional slideshows, which ran in theatres before the feature films. Walter was now associated with moving pictures, soon to be called motion pictures. He was making the animation portion, while most were doing live action. Back at Iwwerks-Disney, Ubbe couldn't last without Walter and soon joined Cauger's organization.

Learning His Craft

Even though the work did excite Walter, it was not up to the mark as far as he was concerned. Though the craft to make pictures look as moving figures was primitive, it was work in progress for him; he was more concerned about learning than earning.

By now he had made his own visiting card stating clearly, 'Contact me for designs, cartoons, illustrations and even window cards.' He had actually fallen in love with making things move. His interest was now in animation. At this point, he rejected an offer of becoming a cartoonist at *The Star*, for which he had been waiting for so long.

By now he was intoxicated by animation, moving pictures, as if gripped by a new passion. He loved the combination of technology and art. He was worldly wise and sharp enough to realize that animation was the new mantra and something very few people knew or had the expertise to get into. Call it the first-mover advantage, Walter wanted to become the best and the most revered in this field.

When passion, vision and hard work come together and get aligned, colossal energy is generated.

It was no less than God's gift: once he loved something, he was able to get totally immersed into it, as if possessed. This is one of the most important qualities of successful people.

Now the only thing that mattered to him was animation. He had the quality of making the best use of whatever he had. All throughout his life, he would never miss an opportunity to learn. Now, he used the slide company as his learning ground, his school for self-education. Cauger gave the freedom to his employees to do things their way, especially to those who were good at their work. Though not really a blue-eyed boy of the boss, Walter had enough freedom to experiment. He was allowed to write and shoot his own adverts, thus saving cost and time of the copy department. For Walter, it was a dream come true.

I always tell my MBA students to not ask for a raise in salary; ask for more work, and the salary will follow. This is one fundamental point for success in any organization. Walter had a bigger aim—learn whatever he could learn at the 'cost' of the organization. How many of us think this way? Very few. He would borrow cameras and equipment to experiment in his spare time—he had that hunger in him to learn.

He wanted a studio for experimenting with his ideas. At that very time, his father decided to come back to Chicago, having lost some money in the venture he had invested in. Since Elias had no way of earning, he wanted to build a garage behind Bellefontaine, the family house where Walter stayed with his siblings. He wanted to rent it, but Walter wanted to build his makeshift studio there and offered his father a rent of five dollars a month—which, according to Roy, he never paid!

This was his first studio—built in his backyard.

He used borrowed camera and lights and other equipment from wherever he could and would spend the whole day working on his drawings and experimenting different ways to achieve his goals.

His family was not sure what would happen to

him professionally—they were not even sure that a job existed in the moving pictures. But Walter wanted to become an animator! In 1920, this field was not even two decades old and obviously had not matured as a professional avenue. Since little technology was available, the entire craft was developed on hit and trial method. The challenge was more to do with technicalities rather than the art and craft.

Things in cinematography and animation appeared to be moving in tandem—the first motion picture dates back to 1888; it was a short silent film titled *Roundhay Garden Scene*. Cinematographic commercial venture was launched in Paris in December 1895 with the screening of 10 short films through projectors, using live cast. Animation was still far behind motion pictures. The basis of all animation is the building up, frame by frame, of the moving picture, using exact timing and choreography of movement and sound. Motion pictures use a camera, sound recording to shoot actual scenes enacted by human actors, which are then recorded on a reel to be projected later on a screen.

Being able to create and animate gave Walter a sense of empowerment, making him feel godlike! In addition, it liberated him from the tightly leashed environment of his home, where his father never allowed them much freedom, be it creative or financial. In his subconscious mind, animation was liberation of sorts. Walter was unstoppable as far his dedication and focus were concerned. He picked up books from libraries for self-study before experimenting. At his workplace, with Cauger, he learnt the traditional animation technique of the cut-out system of animation with moving limbs, but that was not good enough for him.

He wanted to experiment with 'cel' technique, which was real animation. The cel technique process was a bit complex. A storyboard was first created showing the broad concept and direction. After that, artists painted cartoons on celluloid, known as 'cels' in short. These cels were then put together and photographed using a special motion-picture camera. The method allowed animators to repeat certain frames, eliminating the need to draw each individual frame over and over in a sequence of animation.

He learnt from others and approached one Mr McCory who was running an animation school in New York and would meet him whenever he came back to Kansas. He would photocopy whatever little material was available in libraries or other privately owned material. This was the kind of dedication he followed to learn the art and the technique. Since Cauger didn't agree to use cel technique, he ventured on his own and took with him one of his former colleagues.

Now he wanted to do something bigger and approached Mr Newman who had a chain of theatres by now; Walter went to him with a one-minute film. Since the content made people laugh a lot, they called it *Laugh-O-Gram*. Newman saw it and was ready to sign up Walter for making many more such films. Walter was thrilled with his first commercial hit. However, he realized that he had goofed up and quoted a price which was his cost price. Nevertheless, from an apprentice of McCory, he had now become an animator! He needed more hands on the deck, as the process was time-consuming; he then took aspiring cartoonists, promising them experience but no money. It worked and these became very popular. He didn't make a lot of money but got praise and attention—that is what he wanted.

Walter also started making live action movies, where he himself acted in some of the scenes. These were easier to make than animation. Now they were attempting to make longer—around six to seven minutes long—animation films.

The entrepreneur in him wanted a studio for himself. At just 19, it was a far-fetched dream. But he wanted to make it happen. His first fairy-tale movie did not find any backers or buyers. Cauger started thinking that Walter might turn into a competitor soon. Walter, in any case, was very sure that he would not work for anyone as soon as his work started booming commercially.

He made his own company, Laugh-O-Gram Films Inc. Within just two years of his entry into the business, he became the president of the company. Now he owned his own studio, however small. His brother Roy encouraged him all along. Gradually, with many budding artists associating with Walter, Laugh-O-Gram became a community of artists.

Now the Kansas kid was firmly in the saddle, on

a frisky horse and a long dusty road ahead. It was a journey which taught him several lessons as he rode along.

> *'If you feel like there's something out there that you're supposed to be doing, if you have a passion for it, then stop wishing and just do it.'*
>
> —Wanda Sykes

4

The Cartoon Business is Not for Cartoons

'We keep moving forward, opening new doors, and doing new things, because we're curious and curiosity keeps leading us down new paths.'

—Walter Elias Disney

To start a business, especially as a start-up, you need money, and this is the biggest hurdle for an entrepreneur to get going. Walter faced the same challenge. We must remember, it was 1920 and that was the time when bank loans were not easy to get, even in the US. There were no venture capital companies and no angel investors.

The concept of angel investors came into being sometime after the Second World War, when soldiers returned from war keen to start something of their own. Before that money was primarily confined to the rich and wealthy families. Private equity emerged after

1945. The first two venture capital firms in 1946 were the American Research and Development Corporation (ARDC) and J.H. Whitney & Company. Former assistant dean of Harvard Business School, Mr Georges Doriot, was the first person to start thinking on these lines and started ARDC in 1946.

In 1957, ARDC invested $70,000[5] in Digital Equipment Corporation (DEC), which fetched them a valuation of over $355 million[6] after the company's initial public offering in 1968. This is when people in the West started thinking about start-ups and becoming angel investors as there were big profits in this business. In fact, America became a great nation of entrepreneurs for this very reason, and they were far ahead of the rest of the world.

It came much later in India and other developing nations. Even today, it is difficult for a start-up to find investors in India.

Search for an Angel Investor: Kick-Start

Through his uncle Robert Disney, Walter got one Mr John Cowles to invest $2,500, as the latter was looking to invest in some venture that would yield results.[7] The

---

[5]https://bit.ly/3CGpV7U

[6]Bhattad, Rajesh. 'Before Apple, Microsoft, There Was Dec', *THE SALESOPSGUY*, 3 August 2020, https://bit.ly/3q23Mfh. Accessed on 26 March 2022.

[7]Green, Jon. 'The Roots of Animation in Kansas City', JCHS *Journal*, 2014, https://bit.ly/37ugkpd. Accessed on 14 March 2022.

market for cartoons was not very weak, and he wanted some contract to sail through. At around the same time, Walter was also looking for a distributor; he quickly bought some new equipment and started hiring as well. His old colleagues joined him and he also got a business manager and a salesman on board. The market was still not flourishing for animation and cartoons. This is where an entrepreneur succeeds: even when the market is underdeveloped or non-existent, they should have the foresight to see its potential and assess it prudently and correctly. Walter had the team but required some solid work to mark a good start.

The first break he got was not very exciting—making films for churches and schools through a distributor. The distributors were a Tennessee branch of Pictorial Clubs. They offered good money but with strings attached and made it an insipid deal. They offered $11,100 for making six films, but would pay only $100 at the signing of the contract and the rest was to be paid 18 months later at the time of delivery of the films.[8] To Walter, it felt like working for free initially. But he grabbed the opportunity as it was his first break.

Except for Walter, others in the field had very little idea of the craft.

To beat the competition, especially from the animators of New York, he started writing scenarios in detail, which could and did give him an edge over

---

[8]Ibid.

others in quality and finesse. He never compromised on quality. His philosophy was that if they couldn't beat them in size, they could beat them in quality. These were like screenplays and had the names of the animators who were to do each scene marked on the margins. It was a very professional way of getting the job done. They were not making any money, but Walter and his coworkers tried to keep the environment light and happy by cracking jokes and pulling each other's legs. Laughter was compensating for the lack of money. They were learning from books and watching other films, with Walter teaching them the basics of drawing, as he felt they needed some training.

Some Tough Times

Walter was an inefficient manager and also bad at managing finances. He did not have any sense of thriftiness, something that he himself admitted. They were all practically working for free initially and managed to finish four out of six films. Mr Cowles loaned him another $2,500. It was just enough to see them through for a while after which came another trouble—Walter's cheques started bouncing. He was under tremendous pressure to deliver his films with no money to move forward. Everyone was trying to pitch in some money. Walter, though broke, said, 'Let us sit tight because this is the opportunity of a lifetime and I am not going to miss this.'[9] Even during the tough time, he kept his chin up and maintained his enthusiasm and positive attitude. A girl who was working part-time with Walter in those troubled days said, 'He had the drive and ambition of ten million men!' That is what was making the company sail through such difficult times. He even started conducting photoshoots of youngsters to make some money.

A dentist, Mr Thomas McCrum, approached him through the reference of Cowles to make a small movie on dental hygiene and his budget was $500. Walter jumped with joy, but Thomas asked him to come to the institute to sign the deal. Walter had given his only pair of shoes for repair and didn't have $1.5 to pay the cobbler. Thomas agreed to pay the money for Walter to pick up the shoes and thereafter the deal was signed. He took two boys as assistants, whom they paid $10 each and finished the movie.

The Tennessee branch of Pictorial Clubs filed for bankruptcy, and this was the last nail in the coffin.[10] Walter had no money to pay for rent and electricity. Cowles once again came to his rescue and paid their debts. As Walter and his manager picked up a cheque from him to pay the employees, they were tired and both

---

[9]Gabler, Neal. *Walt Disney: The Triumph of the American Imagination*, Vintage; reprint edition, 2007.

[10]DeMarco, Robert. 'Walt Disney Never Filed for Bankruptcy', DeMarco Mitchell, PLLC, 1 July 2018, https://bit.ly/3q4GKnT. Accessed on 14 March 2022.

of them were very hungry. They saw a dollar bill in the gutter and both jumped to grab it. Once the manager got it, he said, 'Walter, we are going to have lunch.'[11]

Hope, Even During the Darkest of Times

Walter was not going to give up. It was time for him to change his strategy and he did exactly that. The first attempt was a fiasco, as he tried to combine jokes with animation and tried to sell it to Universal Pictures. He had done these earlier with his Laffets that were created at Laugh-O-Grams. He edited some and wanted to launch them as a new product. Universal responded that they would not be able to slate these in their present scheme of things.

After this attempt had tanked, Walter tried to come up with yet another creative idea. He wanted to make action-animation combined movies, where cartoon figures and characters entered the real world to interact with real people. He got a cute four-year-old girl named Virginia Davis to play a role in the first of such ventures. And that was called *Alice's Wonderland*. He had no money to pay, so he clinched a deal with her parents that he would pay them 5 per cent of any money the company would receive from this venture. He also managed to convince them to let him use their home

---

[11]Gabler, Neal. *Walt Disney: The Triumph of the American Imagination*, Vintage; reprint edition, 2007.

as the set! Walter was trying to cut corners wherever he could and was taking small favours from anyone he could approach.

They were still frightfully behind schedule, as distributors were getting impatient, and Walter had no money to complete the film. Most of his staff abandoned him because they had not received their salaries. He had to leave the rented premises and start making the entire film on his own. With no money, even managing three meals a day was difficult. The café nearby gave food on credit, but it was limited. All that they did in return was make fancy menu cards. An occasional cake from someone's house could cheer them up. At one point, Walter was so hungry that he wanted to go and eat in a restaurant and tell them in the end that he had no money to pay, but he didn't have the gumption to do so. One day, he had to scavenge for food to fill his stomach. The café owner saw him and extended him credit to buy his meals. As if this was not enough, he had to sleep in his office owing to lack of any appropriate space. He became so thin due to lack of food that people thought he had tuberculosis. Bathing was another problem and for that he had to use the railway station toilets.

Things looked bleak, but Walter still did not lose hope; he had firm faith in his abilities and ideas. Soon, he was broke. Despite facing such hardships at the age of 21, he was yet not prepared to give up and also never complained. He had made Laugh-O-Gram

Studio when he was a minor and, hence, could have escaped the wrath of the law, now that the company was placed into bankruptcy. However, he decided to take the responsibility of his failure entirely upon himself. His older brother Roy told him to leave Kansas City and do something else. Was it his constitution, his attitude or something unusual in his DNA that he continued to walk on the path of his dreams?

In later years, he admitted that he felt that stress was weighing him down and crushing him. Of course, in his heart of hearts, he felt crestfallen and heartbroken, which he never let others know. To him, it seemed that he had let down those who trusted him. He was focused on paying back every cent that he owed to the people who helped him. This is one quality that squarely falls under the domain of honesty and integrity and this is the quality that would earn you respect in society and let you reclaim your honour and others' trust.

Walter had now made up his mind to move out of Kansas. He needed money to go to Los Angeles, which would be his ticket to the tinsel town. He was alone, lonely and broke—he would go to the train station and look at the trains leaving the platforms with tears in his eyes. He was at the mercy of his friends for shelter and food. Through his old contacts, he worked for someone to help them create short films, for which he was paid a few dollars. He collected enough money for the train; he then went to all the people from whom he had borrowed money and handed over all his personal belongings to auction and recover whatever they could.

He had reached the lowest point of his life.

It was time to go, and his friends threw him a nice dinner at their place. A woman there even packed three meals for him so that he would not go hungry on the train. He had one pair of trousers, a shirt, a cardigan, an old cardboard suitcase and nothing else apart from an old raincoat and all his drawings—his treasure. His aunt also gave him an old suit of her son so that he could at least dress up.

It was an emotional, bitter departure. His friends still loved him, and that mattered. Even if he had nothing, he could still hold his head high.

A family friend dropped him at the railway station to catch the train to Hollywood. There was no one else to see him off. He had come alone and he was leaving alone. Later, the biggest claim of the guy who had dropped him off at the station was, 'I took Walt Disney to the station when he went to Hollywood.'[12]

With hope in his heart and ambitions of making it big, he had a feeling that he would be successful.

Thus, a legend arrived in Hollywood.

'My barn having burned down, I can now see the moon.'

—Mizuta Masahide, a seventeenth-century
Japanese poet and samurai

---

[12]Ibid.

5

An Entrepreneur in Action

> *'Timing, perseverance and ten years of trying will eventually make you look like an overnight success.'*
>
> —Biz Stone

The Basal Intoxication

Walter Elias Disney landed in Hollywood, the Mecca of creative exuberance and an acknowledged capital of dreams and imagination. It had all the ingredients of magic, ambition, deceit, greed, competition, money, panache and charm that go into making a potion of success. Having had little to eat over the last several months had made Walter pallid and listless. He looked weak and impoverished in his old, borrowed, shabby, ill-fitting suit. All that he had was hope, reckless passion and *Alice's Wonderland* tucked in his suitcase.

He had to be where the action was—Hollywood Studios—and where creativity was born. It was a place that had the potential of catapulting someone to unimaginable levels if they had it in them. He knew that if he was good, Hollywood would take him places. And he was not wrong. He was desperate to visit the motion picture studios. Walter, through his old contacts and friends, managed to get a pass to get in. This was a place for the mighty moguls of motion pictures. He first visited the Universal City in San Fernando Valley. He kept wandering in the studios and watching the sets, all of which were like a fantasy to him. He even tried to get a role of an extra, and though he managed to bag one, the shoot got cancelled. He wanted to at least become an action director in the tinsel town. He was ready to wander, explore and soak in the feel of motion picture studios. He also explored Metro-Goldwyn-Mayer and the Paramount Pictures Corporation. It was like being in a Circarama. Incidentally, in later days, Walter created the experience of Circarama for his audience with the 360-degree viewing of a film.

He thought of encashing on his only asset—a print of *Alice's Wonderland*—but there were no takers. Though put off by these unproductive encounters in Hollywood, he nevertheless got a visiting card with 'Walt Disney, cartoonist' printed on it. He went back to his old love, a camera which he had bought cheap; it was a second-hand piece, probably funded by his brother. The camera did to him what liquor does to an alcoholic. He rigged it up with an old motor and he was ready for the show. But now came the question: which show? There was no easy answer.

While he was in Kansas, he had been persistent in writing to distributors in Hollywood to sell his *Alice*. However, he only received rejection letters.

Timing Matters

The first and the only female producer those days in Hollywood was Ms Margaret Winkler. She was secretary to Harry Warner of Warner Bros. Warner was a heavyweight in the industry in those days. Margaret was ambitious and young, and had a lot of contacts in the Hollywood circuit because of her position, giving her the opportunity to meet the high and mighty in the film fraternity. Gradually moving up the ladder, she had become one of the leading producers in animation. Walter had approached her through letters from Kansas, but somehow the deal at that time could not get through.

She had, by now, signed up a few contracts with other producers that had gone sour and her business was taking a hit. She wanted some new product to remain afloat and that was the time when Walter approached her again. She called him to meet her, and it worked! *Alice's Wonderland* was screened in October 1923. Though Margaret was pleased, she felt that the quality should be improved. Seeing that marketing costs for a new product would be immense, she knew Walter would not be in a position to negotiate his payment—she was shrewd. He was offered $1,500 for the first six films and $1,800 for the next six.[13] Walter had no way to negotiate and thus bit the bullet.

Nonetheless, he was very excited and could not wait to tell Roy, who was recovering from tuberculosis in a hospital, about the new development. He broke the news and wished him a quick recovery so that the two could get together and discuss their future plans.

Broke as Ever, but With Work to Do

The brothers had no money as always and that was the starting point of discussion. They partly accepted 'beg, borrow or steal' as their mantra—though they didn't steal. They went to every friend, relative, close and not so close, gracious or nasty, even his brother's girlfriend Edna, as they had to collect money to make the films for Margaret. Friends and family trusted them, and that was what mattered. He promised to return money to those he owed. Roy had no experience of animation and did not even have the required skill set. Though he had an artistic bent of mind too, he was never inclined to join his brother in this venture. Knowing how innocent Walter was, Roy simply wanted to ensure he was not cheated or taken for a ride by others and was ready to work for his younger sibling as a manager.

---

[13]Austin, Daryl. 'The Hungarian Immigrant Who Funded Walt Disney', *Newsweek,* 21 December 2019, https://bit.ly/3i7DcNa. Accessed on 14 March 2022.

Walter named their new venture Disney Bros. As their schedule ahead was tight, he got into the production and shooting right away. They bought a camera and looked for places to shoot—this became an experience of its kind for it was the first time he thought he was on the right track. Virginia Davis, the main character, acted as both the male and the female leads. At times, he had to dodge police looking for permits to shoot, which he didn't have, or resort to creating a makeshift background with a bedsheet. The challenge was to synchronize the actions of the actual Alice, Virginia Davis, with that of the cartoon characters. It is now known as 'rotoscoping'.

They were still in need of money. Though not very sure of the venture, Uncle Robert gave them some—$500 in all. They hired a small room at $10 a month, bought a new camera, which to him was the most essential item of his trade.[14] They also rented a small open place for outdoor shoots.

Back then, there were no computer simulations, no sophisticated gadgets and cameras, and, therefore, they had to make do with whatever they had. With a black cloth over his head and looking into the lens, with Alice (Virginia) in the frame, he had to imagine looking at the empty space where he would have to fit in the

---

[14]Korkis, Jim. 'Whatever Happened to Walt's Garage Studio?', *Cartoon Research*, 20 August 2021, https://bit.ly/3JcB7vx. Accessed on 14 March 2022.

cartoons! Back in the studio, he was running it frame by frame, inserting his cartoons and then merging the whole reel into one as if Alice and her cartoon friends were moving in sync. He worked on the animation himself, shot it himself and edited it himself. It was a one-man show, one that only Walter Elias Disney could accomplish.

Alice Goes Live

'Alice's Day at Sea', the first film of the series called *Alice Comedies,* reached Margaret the last week of December in 1923. She sent him his cheque of $1,500, and Walter paid off all his debts at once. He got only 'satisfactory' as a response from Margaret, for which he was not surprised. He knew that it lacked several things. She asked him to pump in more humour and he agreed with her because she was the one who knew what audience wanted. An important lesson for anyone making a product for public consumption: you must take feedback from people who have to sell the product and not create something sitting in an ivory tower, if you wish to succeed. That is the difference between marketing and selling. For a long time, manufacturers of goods produced certain products and asked the sales team to sell it. Gradually, they learnt that before you create a product, you must learn what people want so that you can fine-tune the product accordingly and then manufacture and market it. Thereafter, you also need to continue taking constant feedback from the customers.

Walter did just the same, and yet Margaret was not very happy. In fact, she asked him to redo one of the films all over again. He did it, hired more staff and was also joined by some of his old gang, especially Iwwerks. They also hired Ham Hamilton, who was a very capable animator. This took some load off Walter. But the end product did not see much improvement and Walter knew it. Lack of a good creative team and the growing pressure of work because of the pace at which they were to produce and deliver was also impacting the quality. He had to satisfy his distributor and follow all suggestions that she came up with.

Despite such hurdles, his *Alice* series had managed to convey freedom and empowerment via this young girl, and the overall taste of a fantasy world to the audience. It was a bittersweet success, but things still did not seem to look up.

As if this was not enough, Margaret got married to a guy who took control of her business. Very shrewd, authoritative and an ambitious guy, Charles B. Mintz was not as polite or diplomatic as his wife and would be curt and sometimes rude, even overbearing. He sent her brother to supervise production and tighten the noose further. Walter was being choked. The future legends of Hollywood were still in tatters and living on a few dollars they could pinch out of the system, which was already buckling under a fiscal strain. Mintz wanted better quality but refused to increase the budget. Though Walter was stuck, he still wanted to be the best animator in the business. For that, he again had to borrow from friends and relatives. Things worked out to be a little better this time since the Mintzs were now satisfied but again got him to sign stringer contracts, with tighter financial clauses that were not in his favour. Twenty-six more films of the *Alice* series were signed.

Making Better Films under Pressure

He was bowing to every demand of the Mintzs, and it was infringing on his creativity and also his freedom of doing what he felt was right. He bought new cameras, better motor drive to make filming smoother and also better tripods to mount. In the bargain, he learnt a lot. Walter was producing one film per week! They also hired a cameraman from 20th Century Studios. You need to learn special skills from special people, and Walter said that he learnt a lot from the new cameraman, which benefitted him later.

Now, they had close to 10 people on board and it was a reasonably big team for the Disney Bros. He had always told people joining him from Kansas that they made a big mistake in not coming to Hollywood earlier for this was the place of action and for making it big.

Walter would never compromise on quality and was bending over backwards to accommodate Mintz's suggestions.

Love, Life and Marriage

Walter was not interested in women for the only reason that he did not find them sharing his interests. He was way too involved in his work and not keen on marriage, as he thought it would be binding and would mean losing his freedom. He had made up his mind that he would get married only after he had managed to save $10,000.

Lillian Marie Bounds was an ink artist at Disney Studios and had joined at a measly salary of $15 a week. Born in February 1899, she was a few years older than Walter. She went on to become a big support for her husband through his tumultuous journey, where he needed a sensible and caring partner. Love blossomed gradually when Walter started giving Lillian a ride home from the studio in his car. Though not head over heels in love, they liked each other's company. It was more of a companionship than sheer love.

Was She His Lucky Charm?

It appeared that Lillian was his lucky charm. After their return from their honeymoon, good news awaited them. Reviews of his *Alice Comedies* were not only positive but some of them were even quite encouraging. For instance, Motion Picture World review mentioned, 'Walt Disney cartoons appear to be more imaginative than the preceding one.' There were even talks about creating a book around the concept.

He had to now increase the frequency of delivery of his films—almost one every two weeks. Cash crunch was always a pain for Disney Studios. Distributors maintaining their stranglehold would not easily pay up that fast. Mintz and his wife promised him that they wanted to take his work to the entire world. Walter wanted name and fame, but he needed money too. Though he was gaining popularity, there was still no money.

> *'All our dreams can come true, if we have the courage to pursue them.'*
>
> —Walter Elias Disney

The Cruel World of Cinema

When Walter got a taste of name and fame, he moved his studio to a small bungalow, and that was good enough to give him a sense of achievement. At the same time, certain cost-cutting measures had to be exercised—Virginia, who had been the central actor for the *Alice* series, was turning out to be too expensive. So, Walter decided that she should be paid per day rather than being given a lump sum on a contract. This was not acceptable to her parents, and under pressure from the distributors, he had to replace her with another child artist. At the same time, their cartoons were becoming more and more prominent and better in quality, and were now ready to replace live artists to a large extent.

These are the ways of showbiz: you have no permanent friends, no permanent enemies. Emotions count little in a fiercely competitive environment, where money and fame always rule your decisions. In a creative industry, you need two hearts—one soft and gentle to create, and the other of stone to take or give shit without impacting your health or sleep. I would also like to add that almost a similar situation exists for authors. It is very difficult to get good publishers, especially for a new entrant. Unless you prove your mettle consistently, you are unlikely to remain on the shelf for long.

Even with cash trouble, Walter planned to have a bigger studio, which he wanted to name as Walt Disney Studios, almost becoming the overall commander-in-chief. Roy didn't protest and went along with his decision. On the home front, Lillian was a comforting presence, a good listener and always ready to comply with Walter. Significantly though, his brother admitted that it was difficult for any woman to live with a person as dedicated to his profession and as dominating as he was. She, in fact, worshipped him and went along with things as he wanted. Had she been any different, they would have most likely parted ways. But being from the same craft, she could understand his commitment and his capability, and could add value whenever required.

Working under Pressure

Walter was reeling under pressure. There were two pressure points that made him uneasy. First was that of finances because of the tightening of the fiscal noose by Mintz, and the second was his obsession to produce the best quality on a shoestring budget. He was in a catch-22 situation. He was also very ambitious, wanting to become a big name and that too quickly.

Walter couldn't handle this with finesse. In order to please his own ego and that of Mintz, he started ridiculing, abusing, insulting and harassing his senior coworkers who were also good artists. But if Walter had ego, so did they.

Handling people is the most difficult part of an entrepreneur's journey, and this is mostly what they falter in. A lack of maturity and experience is what causes the discord in most cases. Today, you feel pressurized by your clients, customers and those who fund your start-up. Customers want the best and are adamant about paying very little for the product or service, and your angel investors stop being angels once they risk their money on you. They interfere, cajole, push and even harass you to perform, often with the least budget.

You are left with the feeling that every employee is obliged to give in their 100 per cent, clocking in 24 hours a day, 365 days a week. You may be passionate to the hilt; it is, after all, your core business. Others are just employees; they have other commitments and need time for their personal life. You might be making an empire for yourself, but they are not. Most of them just work for the money. Therefore, an entrepreneur should always care for the people who work for them. You have to be humane and stop comparing their commitment to yours. Remember, it is difficult to get good people to work for you, and it is much more difficult to retain them. This is one quality that cannot be taught in management schools and has a lot to do with emotional intelligence, which most young people may not have developed.

A Broken-Up Team

Walter's coworkers started conspiring against him and were planning to create a rival studio. However, before they could put their work into action, Walter fired them after they were found wanting. Others left too, and people called it a 'hell hole to work in'. These resentments lingered long, as long as it took to break up the organization.

Things started cracking, and it was a serious crisis for the studio. At the same time, Mintz was of the opinion that *Alice* had outlived its charm and time. He wanted the creation of a new character, and Walter started working on it. They had completed 56 *Alices* and were now to shift creative gears.

Along with it came another big opportunity that

Walter could not afford to miss. Mintz had contacted Universal Studios, and they wanted to make it big in the cartoon animation business. They wanted to get a fresh animal character, as there were cats galore in the business. Walter created a funny rabbit, and Universal was to portray this character as 'Oswald the Lucky Rabbit'. He was to prove his mettle and performance to Universal and had to create great cartoons and create them fast. He produced the first one in 15 days. Universal was not happy and refused to release it. This was a big setback for him. Not only were they unhappy with the look of the rabbit, they also could not find a viable storyline. They felt that these were mere strings of jokes and gags without any direction. Universal wanted something more substantial. Walter was of the opinion that cartoon films can't be made as feature films as they were two widely divergent genres. In a way he was right, but Universal was the boss, being the investor.

Long story short, Walter worked hard to satisfy his client, and the funny rabbit was received with good reviews. Oswald the Lucky Rabbit was born and was there to stay. Interesting short stories and ideas were built around the character to help in its sale.

Walter infused his creative competence into his Rabbit, which was noticed not only by the media and critics but also by the audience. His rabbit was more flexible, could be stretched, squeezed, dented, twisted or even inflated or deflated to sync with different funny scenarios. This was the unique selling proposition (USP) of Walter Elias Disney that, in a way, made Oswald the Lucky Rabbit a de facto industry benchmark.

The Lucky Rabbit

Oswald proved to be very lucky for Walt Disney Studios. The financial and creative crisis was almost over. It was time to look after the loyal employees. He also hired new staff, hiked the salary of the old guard—all to ensure that everyone was happy and motivated. Now he had more than 20 people on board. Roy and he were still drawing less than some of the employees, which is yet another lesson for entrepreneurs. Initially, it is best not to draw a big fat salary so as not to drain the system.

They had created some surplus from the profits, after which Walter bought some oil stocks and a piece of land. They still lived in small houses and spent carefully. But for the first time, these two owned their own separate homes. Walter had little time to enjoy this luxury, as he always stayed in the studio. He got his mother-in-law to stay with them to keep his wife company.

Walter loved dogs. He presented a dog to his wife in a rather creative and comical way. He put the pup in a hat box with a ribbon bow on top and gifted it to her. She was delighted with her present and also with the way it was presented to her. This idea was later used as an iconic moment in the animation movie *Lady and the Tramp*. Geniuses get ideas from certain acts, however small they may seem.

Luck Was to Run Out Again

Soon, there was a conspiracy. Mintz was tired of Walter's constant haggling about money and also realized that the actual work of drawing was not done by him, but by some of his well-groomed artists and painters. He wanted Walter to be rendered redundant. Mintz was the man with money, and he bribed and offered Walter's staff to work for him directly. Most of the important staff abandoned him, except Ubbe, who was Walter's most loyal friend. Without informing him, most of Walter's staff went ahead and signed a contract with Mintz.

Walter approached Mr Fred Quimby of Metro-Goldwyn-Mayer, but he said he was not interested in cartoons for, he thought, they were on the wane. Now, Walter had been reduced by Mintz to a sub-contractor level. He was back to square one, with no authority and no rights to his creations. He learnt yet again that Hollywood was full of deceit and unscrupulous people—one could not trust anyone. The biggest concern for Walter was that he had to start all over again.

He was on a train back home with Lillian, whom he had so enthusiastically taken to New York to ink a deal with Mintz. He was devastated and felt let down by his own staff and also by Mintz. He swore to himself that from then on, he would not work for anyone and would create something of his own. They had run out of money and were only left with a reputation that Walter had built for his work. He was now more worldly wise with his hard-earned experiences.

Meanwhile, Lillian worried over how they would survive, seeing that they had no money. For a young entrepreneur who is single, life is difficult enough. If they have a family to look after, life can be miserable. The husband-wife duo had an eerie feeling on their train back home.

However, a mouse was yet to be born.

> *'It's fine to celebrate success, but it is more important to heed the lessons of failure.'*
>
> —Bill Gates

6

A Mouse is Born

> *'Walt Disney was a master of the human psychology. His sense of timing, sense of speed. In a sense, those cartoons are like Rorschach tests.'*
>
> —Twyla Tharp

Life for Walter Elias Disney, till now, had been fast, fierce and furious. He had tasted defeat in more than one way. At first, it was in Kansas City, where he gave his best shot and couldn't make the cut, and then his move to Hollywood with all the hope and twinkle in his eyes turning out to be another fiasco. Hollywood left him with deceit, betrayal and failure.

Dejected and demoralized, Walter felt cheated by the people he trusted to a large extent. Annoyed with his luck and failure of catastrophic proportions, he had hundreds of crazy and not-so-happy thoughts running through his head while he was on the train back home to Los Angeles with Lillian on 13 March 1928.

One thing was now clear to him: whatever he would create from then on, he would keep the rights with himself. He had created something, and it was snatched from him by greedy and shrewd distributors. He felt that perhaps due to his desperation to associate with a distributor, he had inadvertently gone wrong when he signed the dotted line with Margaret. But never again. This was a lesson he would never forget in his life, a lesson learnt a very hard way.

For an artist, his art is the biggest stressbuster. Walter started sketching some characters on paper and building a storyline all at once. He felt that he had left his Alice and her wonderland—a major part of his body and soul—behind when he boarded the train. For a creative person, what can be more demeaning than this? He struggled to keep his composure. Lillian saw him, for the first time, being upset and raging like a wild animal. He wanted to replace Oswald the Lucky Rabbit maybe as an act of trying to get rid of all the bad memories.

He then came up with the idea of a mouse that could be given life and blood to make for an interesting character.

He thought of a crazy mouse who builds his own airplane to impress a lady mouse. Around this, he spun a short story. He started sketching some figures on paper to put clarity to his thoughts and figure out a character that would make sense.

He named the mouse 'Mortimer'—a rather weird

name. He turned to his wife and narrated the plot. On a train journey that had just begun after a disastrous closure of sorts, she was in no mood to listen to Walter talk about his cartoons yet again. When he told her that the name of the mouse would be 'Mortimer', she got further annoyed. What kind of a name was that? She thought it was too silly. Most of the time, creativity and its acceptance work instantly or not at all. You either like it or you don't, there is no thoughtful consideration or deliberation about it. On top of it, it is difficult to say why you like something or why you don't. For example, let's say you like red and hate blue—there can be no logical reason for it. That is why, in show business, it is very difficult to judge what the audience might like or not.

> *'Of all of our inventions for mass communication, pictures still speak the most universally understood language.'*
>
> —Walter Elias Disney

Mickey Mouse

'Mortimer' was a no go. Walter agreed to an extent and came up with another name in an instant. How about Mickey, he asked? Lillian found it better than Mortimer, and that is how Mickey Mouse was born and baptized—on a train. A legend had just created another!

As they reached Los Angeles, Walter was not his usual self—bubbly, enthusiastic and energetic—as anyone who knew him would have imagined. Under normal circumstances, he would have been jumping with joy after creating a new character like Mickey Mouse. But the circumstances were far from normal for him for he had hit the lowest point in life.

There was no choice but to start once again and rebuild everything. It required bootstrapping, getting his faculties into working mode and letting the creative juices flow once again. Walter and Roy were back in action. They scanned through what all had been done by other artists and creative masters in the field of animation. This particularly involved looking at which animal characters had been drawn and which ones were being liked by the audience.

This is an important part of the creative process. You cannot be sitting in an ivory tower creating something in isolation without understanding the market condition. The same is true for authors; they must understand what is trending and also find the gap that has to be bridged. Walter, Roy and Ubbe were doing just that. They were laboriously sifting through newspapers and magazines.

Walter was very impressed by the works of Clifton Meek, an artist of his times who ran a comic strip in the *Life Magazine* and also drew comic strips for Newspaper Enterprise Association, titled 'Johnny Mouse'. He particularly liked the mouse drawn by

Clifton. Walter understood that the mouse could be the central character in his future animation films.

Both Ubbe and Walter started working on creating a mouse, which would be distinct and also look cute. They came up with several versions, rejecting many of their own creations as they were not satisfied. Finally, they came up with a mouse with a pear-shaped body, round ears, a nose pointing in the air, rather thin legs, arms, hands and wearing big shoes. It had a round figure which would be easier to animate than any other shape.

They were yet under contractual obligation to deliver films on Oswald to Mintz. At the same time, they were working on their next character, Mickey Mouse. Walter had limited staff that remained loyal to him; they were catering to huge pressure, with two projects running parallel. The mouse was being created in utmost secrecy so that no one could steal their idea. This was their trade secret and rightly so as later this went on to become a fulcrum of sorts for their studio. They mostly worked at night, when others had gone home. They were yet to find takers for Mickey and sign a contract.

Everyone in the staff worked for free when there was no money for their salaries; they ate frugally and managed to live by on their own. It was a matter of survival for the studio.

Walter wanted to sell Mickey and bring it to the market as soon as possible and hence went to theatres displaying Mickey short films. People applauded the films, but there were still no takers.

'Making cartoons means very hard work at every step of the way, but creating a successful cartoon character is the hardest work of all.'

—Joseph Roland Barbera

The Sound of Music

Walter had another bright idea—to introduce sound to moving Mickey. This was a great idea, but the team felt awkward trying to decipher how people would react to sound coming from a cartoon figure. Sound was making entry into films at that point, but those films had human characters. The next challenge ahead was non-availability of technology for synchronizing cartoons with music and voice-over, and figuring out how to work around it.

He started from the basics and got Jackson, the youngest from his team, to work on it, as he was the only one who knew something about music. They decided that synchronization would be done frame by frame.

One night, Walter had all the contraptions in place. He had set up the projector, which was to throw images on a white bedsheet in the open space in the studio backyard, with Jackson playing the music in sync, frame by frame, on his musical instrument. The audience consisted of friends and family, and they loved it. It worked, and they had done what no one had done till then. This was innovation at its best—the synchronization of sound and light in the most primitive way.

Though the outcome was poor in quality, it proved that it could be done and the audience would be mesmerized. They raised more funds and got hold of someone who could put a soundtrack on the celluloid film. They were sitting on a revolution as of now that was on the verge of becoming iconic.

They wanted a professional well-versed with new technology. Mr Powers had developed cinephone, a technology that put sound on the side margins of the film and could be read by a pickup head to project sound and light perfectly.

Walter hired a recording studio, and the first recording was a disaster—he was down by $1,000. He was very disturbed and couldn't sleep or eat. Powers was looking at long-term gains and managed the recording studio with Walter paying for the musicians. They had to take out a loan again. Walter knew that it had to work or otherwise they would be doomed. This time, he went ahead with a ball painted on both the soundtracks that rose and fell to the beat. It worked very well. *Steamboat Willie*, the first film starring Mickey Mouse with synchronized sound was made. Again, there was a hunt for a producer, but no one was coming forward to take on the distribution. Walter was stuck again—he was crushed financially, and his morale was shattered. How much can a man take? He had tried his best and put everything on the line—his home, his work, his reputation. He finally sold his car to raise the money. He had four films of Mickey Mouse—all with sound—and no takers. He was losing his confidence now. He had run out of patience and was exasperated.

Sometime then, Walter came across a person who had experience of selling pictures and had become the manager for Colony Theatre, and he agreed on screening his films there. He was Harry Reichenbach, the man who came to his rescue.

On 18 November 1928, *Willie* was screened. Though barely six minutes in length, it was applauded by the audience and the media alike. It became a rage, and soon Walter was moving forward, perhaps for the first time in his life. Others tried to make cartoons with sound, but he was far ahead and had the first-mover advantage. Hollywood distributors wanted to buy not only his cartoons but the studio as well. Walter didn't want to part with his studio and was determined to keep it with him at all cost.

Powers was a scheming fellow with a dubious past record, and Walter had, unfortunately, fallen into his trap.

Powers was the one getting distributors and had connections and the expertise to sell.

Not one to take a backseat, Walter now wanted to get into sound production, as that seemed to be the key to success, and, at that point, their weakness or shortcoming. He wanted to be the king of animation. Powers was smart; he helped him in every possible way to set up a recording studio, but signed him for a fat royalty. Roy objected, but by then it was late and Walter was desperate to conquer the sound industry. He had made several such decisions in desperation in the past and any entrepreneur can take a lesson from this. Never sign before taking sound advice from someone who knows commercial math.

Master of Ceremony

Now Walter had control over both sound and light. They also created another first, sound trucks for outdoor shooting.

He wanted to go ahead and create some more characters, as he knew Mickey alone won't do. He was always running on parallel tracks, at the same speed andwith the same enthusiasm. He learnt to hedge his risks and not put all his eggs in one basket.

He was obsessed about getting the right talent on board, whatever the cost. He got top-rated animators from the market, hired them and got them inducted in the system at the earliest, as he was expecting to make 36 new cartoons that year. This was another strategic move. Some of the best cartoonists of the time, like Ben Sharpsteen, were hired at a salary more than what Walter and Roy were drawing individually.

Picking up the right talent is one of the most important jobs of an entrepreneur. 'Hiring guys better than you' is the mantra. No wonder that start-ups today are getting talent from IITs and IIMs and paying them big salaries.

Hiring a bungalow at a low price in Los Angeles was another move. There, they made space for all departments, including painting, inking, recording and sound. Several things were of the makeshift kind but were under the same roof. Workspace was frugal, but it worked well.

> *'Mickey represented an honest product, a pure spirit and a cheerful heart, a sort of staggeringly simple pleasure in the exercise of the imagination.'*
>
> —Eve Zibart

The Devil's in the Detail

Though the space looked haphazard, the work was done meticulously. Every cartoon character had a written exposure sheet that outlined each scene and each movement exactly as it was supposed to go. Walter had an eye for detail and stayed professional—that is what made him Walter Elias Disney. Everyone in the studio was convinced that the devil's in the detail and they worked towards it.

It was not the quality of work alone, but the benchmark of expectation of delivering the best—this formed the core of his success mantra. Walter had to be the best and nothing less. Excellence, finesse and perfection was to go into every scene, every frame, without any compromise at all. The most difficult part of his job was to motivate the workers and artists to change their mindset as at that time cartoon business was not taken seriously.

He possessed a great quality to inspire commitment with his own passion and dedication towards his craft. He almost worshipped his work and it was written all over his face. The one thing everyone who wants to succeed in a big way must remember is this: work towards the best product and money will come automatically like a by-product Ubbe said, 'We would hate to go back home and would love to come back early next morning.'[15] If you can create such an environment, then you are the king in the truest sense, and Walter Elias Disney had arrived as king of animation. However, this came with many setbacks—hard work, deceit, harassment and plenty of failures. The atmosphere at work remained relaxed, with people cracking jokes or pulling pranks. This, however, never impacted the aim for excellence at work.

Walter had learnt the hard way how to deal with his artists and staff. He had been too harsh in his earlier days and couldn't underplay the mutiny of his staff against him, having lost them to his competitor. Now he mended his ways; given his financial condition

---

[15]Gabler, Neal. *Walt Disney: The Triumph of the American Imagination,* Vintage; reprint edition, 2007.

was better, he put in some extra effort to create a relaxed workspace. His staff appreciated the move and was happy to work at Disney Studios.

Good quality costs money, and again, the financial strain started impacting the studio. Walter was never to compromise on quality and paid his staff well. Producing the best quality of films was becoming more and more expensive. His sound recording studio was yet to rake in any profits. He had to pay off his earlier debts too. But he could just about manage to stay afloat.

Raking in More Money

When you desire perfection, you may run out of money, especially in show business. Movie-making business is famous for going over-budget. Disney Studios was facing the same trouble, as Walter was pushing the envelope of excellence. The only way was to sign up more cartoons with a big distributor. Metro-Goldwyn-Mayer was a giant, and Walter tried his luck with them. Though the initial response was positive, the deal could not be closed. He went to Columbia Pictures and started towards making it big. It worked, and he signed a contract, which meant a regular flow of funds.

Bitter experience with Mintz was still at the back of his mind, and Walter was not happy with money alone for he wanted control and domination. The only rival for Mickey Mouse was Felix the Cat and its creator Pat Sullivan. Mickey was well-entrenched in the market and had sound as its USP. Pat was lagging behind with silent cartoons. He couldn't catch up with Walter's finesse and craftsmanship in terms of both sound and picture quality. He was gradually made irrelevant and was no more a competition, forget being a threat to Walter.

Marketing Mantra

As luck would have it, almost at the same time, Harry Woodin, manager at a studio in Los Angeles, created a Mickey Mouse Club on his own. He would invite children to be a part of this club, and every Saturday, kids used to take a Mickey pledge! It was a wholesome experience. He invited Walter, who immediately understood the potential of this activity. They tied up to do this on a national level. They started a Mickey Mouse national campaign, and it made Mickey Mouse the biggest thing in the cartoon industry. There were pie-eating competitions, games and other props related to Mickey in abundance. Kids loved the matinee show, and parents were happy packing them off to these shows to get almost half a day of respite. Everything was falling in place.

This is what one should learn from the Americans. They are great at marketing, and they do it in a big way. They consult, conceive and collaborate. It is also important to understand that your product must be good too. Good marketing cannot sell a bad product, but an excellent product will fail if it is not marketed properly. It is more important today because of the fierce competition prevailing in the market.

Branding Mickey and Minnie, the Mice

Merchandise like buttons, badges, toys and banners were created with Mickey riding high. These also generated a steady revenue stream with vendors, merchants and Disney—everyone earning and sharing the profits. There was a Mickey Mouse creed that Mickey Mouse does not smoke, does not swear or lie. There was a social message in this, which all parents and media appreciated. Kids loved Mickey. A special Mickey song, akin to a Mickey anthem was created which kids sang. It was titled 'Minnie's yoohoo', and at the end of every club session, this was sung by everyone.

It went like this:

> I'm the guy they call little Mickey Mouse
> Got a sweetie down in the chicken house,
> Neither fat nor skinny
> She's the horse's whinny
> She's my Minnie Mouse!

With this, not only Mickey but his girlfriend Minnie also got an image boost.

Very soon there were more than 800 chapters of the club across America, with more than a million fan members. It was a larger number than even those of the Boy and Girl Scouts put together. Then they created a

Mickey Mouse comic strip, which gave it a further fillip.

In marketing, if you want to succeed, you must resort to carpet bombing, and that is what was done by Disney Studios. All guns were blazing simultaneously. That is how a cult is created. It was running very soon in more than 20 countries and in over 40 newspapers, making Mickey Mouse an international celebrity, larger than its creator, Walt Disney!

> *'Times and conditions change so rapidly that we must keep our aim constantly focused on the future.'*
>
> —Walter Elias Disney

Creating Collaterals

Now was the time to further encash on his mouse. Walter wanted to give a boost to Mickey Mouse merchandise in a big way. The time was right, but he could not do it himself, as neither did he have the time, nor did he have the expertise to make and distribute at a national level. They started talking to manufacturers for Mickey candies, Mickey toys and also Mickey comics.

Once a product achieves some amount of success, things start happening on their own. They were now being sought after by big guys like Metro-Goldwyn-Mayer, Paramount and so on. Roy and Walter were on a high. They were now on the other side of the fence. For the last several years, the duo had been on the receiving end, defensive most of the time and struggling to get a foothold amongst the greats. Studios had never treated them as equals, and Walter wanted to become the first among equals.

The Second Mini Coup

Ubbe who was drawing all the Mickeys was not getting his due in terms of recognition and did not want to live under the wings of Walter any more. He was not happy with the micromanagement that Walter was prone to do. Perhaps it was too much interference, being sidelined in public and getting no visible credit for his contribution that made him leave Disney Studios.

The guy who gave sound and music to Walt Disney cartoons, Carl Stalling, also felt something similar and quit Walter's team almost at the same time. Walter, obviously, was unhappy. But it must be understood that if Walter wanted to be famous, so did the others. Yet another way of looking is that it was Walter, as the entrepreneur, who put his neck in the noose for two decades and mortgaged everything that he ever had to reach where he did. Ubbe and Carl were working for a salary with no risk or pressure involved. The guy who gets the shots also calls the shots.

Every entrepreneur has to be careful in this regard: do not allow your employees to get into your head and make you feel like they are equal stakeholders of the company. Remember, you had an idea and you implemented it, taking all the risk, while the others worked with you for a salary.

Though hurt emotionally, this coup was not going to hurt the business, as by now, things were in place and there was no shortage of money.

At the same time, Walter was very naïve and trusted people easily, and this time it was Powers whom Roy could never trust. Powers could turn the tables any time and Roy had warned his younger brother about it. The first act of breach of trust by Powers was to hire Ubbe. At the same time, he was shooing away prospective distributors who were approaching Walter with a threat that he would sue Disney Studios for breach of contract if they ditched him. Metro-Goldwyn-Mayer and Columbia Pictures, therefore, refrained from making a deal with Walter, and he was now trapped again.

It was a legal war with Powers and in the end, with support from Columbia Pictures, they could get out of his stranglehold, but at a big price as they had to pay him for settlement. In this lies another lesson for start-ups—try to avoid getting someone on board to help you by giving them the rights to your product. As you become big, you are sure to be arm-twisted.

Mickey Mouse was back in the game and so was Walter. Columbia Pictures gauged the potential of the Mouse and that is why, they helped Walter extricate himself from the hold of Powers. Mickey Mouse was now a rage across the US and the entire Europe. So much so that he had a larger presence on the hoardings. Austrians were worried thinking Mickey was becoming a larger figure than Mozart.

You have actually arrived when people start imitating you. This happens with actors and singers too. Mickey was being cloned, copied and imitated by others in the cartoon business. Though good for popularity, Walter had to go to court against such copycat ventures by others.

Mickey was a soothing balm to the Americans during The Great Depression in the '30s.

> *'Laughter is timeless, imagination has no age, dreams are forever.'*
>
> —Walter Elias Disney

Mickey Analysed

When something becomes a great success, people start analysing the reasons behind it. Mickey was being analysed by several experts in the creative and intellectual fields. What made Mickey Mouse the Mickey Mouse?

The simple explanation and observation in *Time Magazine* in the year 1933 was that this mouse symbolized freedom and simplicity. He was so innocent and his pranks so very genuine. He could break all laws of nature—gravity, twistability, elasticity, tenacity, flexibility—sometimes with a hardened exterior, being soft on the inside. But he never broke any moral laws. He lived in the moment, forgot bad stuff easily and was back in form within a second. He was rather adventurous and a bit scandalous in a cute way.

Facelift of the Studio

The old bungalow was now given not only a facelift but also some extra space to accommodate more staff. There was a neon sign that displayed 'Walt Disney' with a five-foot-tall Mickey Mouse proudly donning the rooftop. A sense of regimentation and camaraderie was palpable.

Price of the Mouse: Home Alone

His work was keeping him busy almost round the clock, and this made Lillian very lonely. He was always immersed in his work, right from the beginning of their relationship. But now he was getting obsessed with mouse, cat, squirrels, ducks, animals, themes, anecdotes, plots—it was never ending. She was now getting bored of his stories, especially since Mickey Mouse became the latest phenomenon he was obsessed with in his heart and mind.

One person's obsession could turn into another's bane. That is the greatest dichotomy of creativity, and it happens to authors, directors, actors, musicians, singers, instrumentalists, poets, painters, lyricists and other creative people. It happens to all of them in different degrees.

Though Walter wanted to spend time with his family, his cartoons possessed him. He would go from theatre to theatre to watch his cartoons and check the audience's response. As compensation, Walter used to take his wife for a drive, only to remember midway that there was some urgent work at the studio that needed his attention. Lillian said, almost every time, they would end up at the studio late at night.

He was now around 30. Lillian felt he refused to grow up.

> *'That's the real trouble with the world. Too many people grow up.'*
>
> —Walter Elias Disney

The Business Ahead

Walter had, by then, learnt not to trust the distributors, be it Columbia Pictures. He planned his future moves carefully like a preemptive strategy. He was already in talks with United Artists, a big name then, well before the Columbia Pictures contract was about to expire. It was done with utmost discretion, and that is also a lesson for every start-up or even those who have been in business for ages: keep your cards close to yourself to avoid any espionage or ambush.

He also suspected that Columbia Pictures was not delivering as promised in terms of marketing and profits. United Artists later said that Mickey Mouse was the greatest star ever produced in motion picture history.

Despite arm-twisting tactics by Columbia Pictures, which was still distributing Mickey before the contract expired, Walter kept his cool and refused to be pressurized in any way. For him, his studio was a sacred place, a temple of wisdom and creativity, and he stood like a mighty Rock of Gibraltar between his artists and the outside pressure. This was one reason behind his humungous success and a lesson in leadership and commitment, which all those in any business must understand and implement to the hilt.

He worked not for money but for quality, perfection and for being the best in the business.

The Price of Success

Walter was pushing himself too hard. He was also pressing his artists to draw fast and draw better. Yet his enthusiasm was not as it used to be. He was, in fact, falling apart.

Now unable to sleep, he used to sometimes cry without any reason while talking to people. He was stressed to the limit but refused to let go of his obsession. He should have known where to draw the line. He was in a downward spiral of his own making, and it was sucking his peace of mind.

Finally, he had to see a doctor, who advised him to move away from work.

What he thought to be emotional stress was actually a nervous breakdown. Mickey's creator was now sick and suffering.

> *'Success is not final, failure is not fatal: it is the courage to continue that counts.'*
>
> —Winston Churchill

7

Fall and Rise of Walt Disney: The Birth of Cartoonism

'I only hope that we never lose sight of one thing—that it was all started by a mouse.'

—Walter Elias Disney

Walter always had symptoms of a manic-depressive. With every project he started, his condition aggravated because of his obsession with perfection. Mickey Mouse was a great success and the best thing to happen to Disney Studios, yet he was irritated all the time. His family and colleagues observed that his moods moved in a cyclic fashion. They swung between episodes of manic creativity, followed by severe depression, anxiety or nervous exhaustion. To add to this, his obsession to make the best always pushed his films beyond the budget and that led to shortage of funds, making his condition worse.

Was perfection at work the only reason for his nervous breakdown? No. He had also suffered a personal tragedy. Walter loved children, so much so that he had once mentioned to his sister Ruth that he wanted to have 10 children; he wanted to give them a happy childhood, which he had never experienced for himself. Lillian and Walter wanted to start a family. In the spring of 1931, Lillian was pregnant, and Walter was thrilled. But, as destiny would have it, she suffered a miscarriage. This left Walter devastated; he had all the success, but he had lost his child. Instead of going for a holiday and taking a break, he immersed himself in his work with much more ferocity than before. That impacted him adversely and he suffered a breakdown.

His life itself moved like a sinusoidal wave with sharply opposing crests and troughs. In all, he suffered about eight bouts of nervous breakdowns during his illustrious, somewhat tumultuous career, where at times he was riding the crest of popularity, praise and receiving Oscars and accolades and yet at other times, fighting for his very survival. Such was the life of this creative genius.

Despite all this suffering, he had managed to create a fascinating body of work that was adored by children and adults alike.

The Great Depression

As if Walter's personal mental health issues were not troublesome enough, America suffered its greatest economic slowdown and the stock markets crashed in October 1929. It had a domino effect that rippled across the world, and no country could escape its tremors. This was known as The Great Depression. It was remembered as a black Tuesday. The film industry, too, was not spared by this raging bull and it hit those who had invested big in buying theatres in the 1920s. Property values crashed and they had no assets so to speak that could be used. Many others in the industry who had invested in stocks also saw their money getting wiped out. Disney Studios was not affected because they had no real estate in the real sense! Apart from their films in cans and a studio, they had a couple of small land parcels. They had ploughed back all their earnings into their own studio and hence cheated the Depression in a way. If you were poor, you were better off in such times.

In this economic breakdown, Walter was fighting his family as well as mental health issues. He, along with Lillian, planned a vacation that did him a lot of good. He returned to the studio, fully rested and charged. He had now at last understood that life had to be lived and there was something outside of work too. He wanted to virtually extend his hassle-free holiday by opting for some sports or outdoor activity. Horse riding was something he had always wanted to do, and now he took it up as a break away from work. He also joined the Hollywood athletic club—a kind of a gym in those days—where he became a regular at swimming and even wrestling.

He started playing golf during morning hours pretty regularly. Roy wanted his younger brother to continue living a more relaxed life so that he could recover and also learn to live. He took more responsibility on himself and soon, during the Depression itself, he signed a contract with United Artists to produce films. He also managed a hefty loan so that Walter could feel at ease and use it for his creative escapades.

The Expectation Syndrome

Walter continued suffering from a professional syndrome of sorts. He had first suffered at the hands of perfectionism and the pace of production, and now he was hit by another problem—of expectations. He had already established himself as the king of cartoonism—an ism created by himself in his own mind. He had inadvertently raised the bar for himself. Some may call it self-inflicted injury, some may call it insanity, but he looked at it as plain professionalism and being loyal and faithful to his craft.

At Walt Disney Studios, they were pioneers in their craft, and most of the basics of the animation industry, as seen today, emerged from there. This was endorsed by none other than Chuck Jones, one of the finest animators and producers at Warner Brothers. Walt Disney Studios, under the guidance and leadership of Walter, along with its impeccably assembled team of brilliant animators, painters and artists, was conquering new frontiers of creativity. They analysed, discussed, dissected and, sometimes, decimated a product in an iterative way to eliminate all possibilities of anything going wrong. It had to be nothing less than a 100 per cent.

Walter's dictum was that whatever they produce should be such that it could not be improved upon by anyone, including himself. What a brilliant goal by a brilliantly insane creator! No wonder that till date, he commands that respect and acceptability from the audience—his cartoons are the very best. Imagine the difficulty of making perfect pictures in the days when cameras were not what they are today and technology per se was in its nascent stage.

Walt Disney Studios had made a standard operating procedure to be followed for every product, which later became a de facto animation industry standard. They ran rough pencil drawings first, which were then corrected and redrawn till they were perfect. They shot these and ran through them sitting in 'sweat box' to see the rushes, and made notes to improve the content, redraw and repaint to get a final thumbs up from four to five people on the team.

We all have been amazed at the way Disney cartoons glide and flow. There are no jerks and the movements are so very perfect. This was the hardest thing to achieve, and on the insistence of Walter, they devised a method called 'overlapping action'. This was something like superimposing images in rapidity. This was Walter's trademark technique, which was used for very cartoon.

His cartoon films made sense and they were based on short comic situations. There was a narrative to follow, a short storyline—a sequence of events cleverly knitted together. There was a feel and a purpose behind every action. These were pristine and holy in the sense of the craft. Walt Disney Studios was a temple of cartooning and everyone felt so working in that team. This was the culture of perfectionism created by Walter's leadership and his commitment to his craft.

Now, Walter wanted a proper story and each story to have several comic situations: a string of situations to create a proper full-fledged storytelling. So, it was a bottom-up approach, starting with short situations that graduated to full-fledged stories. From there, he moved towards making them more real such that the audience connected with each cartoon and action at an emotional level. His cartoons did not beat the laws of nature but bent them. And this created that excitement; people wished in their heart of hearts that they could be as free and flexible as his characters.

You improve with training. He took his artists for training to one of the best cartoonists. Very soon, Walter created his own art studio, California Institute of the Arts.

Adding Some Colour to His Creatures

There is a world of difference between colour and black-and-white films. Imagine trying to see Donald

Duck or Mickey Mouse in black and white today. It will be unwatchable and unacceptable. Can you imagine watching a National Geographic programme that shows life underwater in black and white? It will be absolutely insipid.

But in those days, people had no choice and had to put up with black-and-white films; Walter wanted to change this. He wanted his audience to have the experience of watching his creatures in colour. He could understand and gauge the impact a colour cartoon film would have on the audience, making animation feel real.

He gave voice to his mouse himself; he gave voice to Mickey Mouse from 1928 to 1947. Later, there were several people who gave voice to the great Mickey.

His next destination was making films in colour. Those days, colour technology was at its nascent stage and also prohibitively expensive, almost unaffordable for a commercial venture of substantial scale.

Technicolor was a company that dealt with colour films, and this was the year 1932. Walter was all for it, but was told by Roy that it would cost them three times more than a black-and-white film. Production costs would also shoot up. They had no one to back it, as their contract with United Artists was only for black-and-white films, and they were not going to change it, as the chances of recovering money were minimal.

Walter became adamant. He was already making an animation film with trees—two trees falling in love and a third one, a spoilsport, coming in between their romance. He shifted midway to contact Technicolor, which was finding it difficult to sell colour to mainstream cinema because of the steep cost. They were losing money and had invested heavily in R&D. They tried to help Walter, who used recycled films and all other cost-cutting techniques to make coloured trees in his latest venture. The greats of Hollywood were fascinated by it. Orders started pouring in. The movie titled *Flowers* and *Trees* got an Academy Award for best animated short film.

'So, that's it,' exclaimed Walter, and he was now hooked to colour just as he was earlier to sound. He wanted everything in colour. For Roy, it was plain silly. But Walter being Walter wanted to go ahead with it anyway. Whether United Artists compensated or not, he was determined to do it. He approached Technicolor for exclusive rights for their process. This was a clever move, but had it backfired, Disney Studios would have had a major failure at hand. Roy and Walter went to them to close the deal, and Technicolor was more desperate to sign the deal than the Disney brothers themselves. No one was knocking on their door to ask for colour.

The duo showed creative wisdom; to understand the impact of a never-tested technology and how to harness it into your product. Walter's genius was his ability to understand the psyche of his audience and that is the ultimate prowess in show business.

When things are meant to work, help comes from all directions. Technicolor was ready to pump in close to $200,000 to finance the Walt Disney Studios and asked for 50 per cent shareholding.[16]

Walter and Roy politely refused. A lesson they had learnt earlier paid off. Walter offered to make 13 Silly Symphony cartoon films in Technicolor, with exclusive rights for using it for two years, as if they were giving Technicolor a chance to showcase their product. This was good enough to exploit the first-mover advantage. It would have paid off eventually, but again their finances were tight.

> *'I'd say it's been my biggest problem all my life...it's money. It takes a lot of money to make these dreams come true.'*
>
> —Walter Elias Disney

Another Hunt for Dollars

Poor Roy was again in a spin and was tasked to raise money. The good old brother started in all earnestness. United Artists was not interested in investing more for colour and was having doubts about the quality consistency of Disney Studios.

Roy had to look elsewhere, and he found Bank of America coming to their rescue. They were even prepared to repay the loan extended by United Artists

---

[16]Gabler, Neal. *Walt Disney: The Triumph of the American Imagination*, Vintage; reprint edition, 2007.

and finance the whole project on their own. Such great organizations like Bank of America were one of the major reasons why entrepreneurs flourished in America, and ultimately it went the capitalist way. It was one Dr Attilio Giannini at Bank of America who believed in character than collateral and could gauge that Disneys would deliver, come what may. He backed them, and now Walt Disney Studios could take loans as they wished. This was a boost for Roy and Walter; they could now move at a faster pace and also deliver quality.

Three Little Pigs

Walter was a master crafter; Disney Studios now created *The Three Little Pigs*. The plot centred around three pigs who were terrorized by a ferocious wolf and how they managed to deal with him.

Robert Fred Moore was a brilliant animator at Disney Studios; he could pump life into a character like nobody else. He had the knack for creating visuals that looked very charming. Walter tasked him to take on the pigs, and he created charming, chubby, rounded pigs that anyone would adore. With smooth movement, came along a song that also became an anthem of sorts. Walter had suggested that a song should be created to back the entire theme—pigs had to be somewhat brave. 'Who's Afraid of the Big Bad Wolf?' was composed by Frank Edwin Churchill, who was the official composer of Disney Studios. This created a rage in America and found its place in musical history. Such tunes are hard to get and hard to forget too.

Shortly after the release of the film, the song was being hummed and whistled by all of America. It was everywhere; it was all over on the radio, newspapers, being sung in bars, in schools, on the streets. *New York Herald Tribune* said, 'You cannot escape it.' At the same time, the demand for the film became too much to handle for United Artists, which was running short of prints. This was Disney Studios' iconic moment. It won Walter another Academy Award. Charlie Chaplin applauded his creativity and performed on the stage for him, which he rarely did. With *The Three Little Pigs,* a new era had begun, that of personality animation.

It helped Walter attain a name and fame that spread worldwide; it went viral in those days when there was no social media. It got him money at last—a whopping \$600,000[17]—besides getting a status of first amongst the firsts. He had not only achieved great heights in animation, but also created a cultural shift. This was happening when the world, especially America, was in the eye of the raging Depression! And because of the Depression, Walter could hire the best animators, composers and musicians. There is always, as they say, a silver lining in a dark cloud.

---

[17]Gabler, Neal. *Walt Disney: The Triumph of the American Imagination,* Vintage; reprint edition, 2007.

By now, Walt Disney Studios had more than 200 employees. It was not labour but intellectual sweat that each one brought to the table. Though it resembled an assembly line, every man in the line was adding phenomenal value to it. This was craft moving in the best and the fastest way. For a normal man, it would have appeared chaotic, but it was a highly organized chaos for the studio.

> *'Get a good idea and stay with it. Dog it, and work at it until it's done right.'*
>
> —Walter Elias Disney

Organizing Intellectual Chaos

Walter's next move was to make the process of creativity as rational as possible so that there were clearly defined and demarcated boundaries of responsibilities. It was still a flat organization because each individual's inputs were as important as those of anyone else in the chain.

There were departments wherein each had to play a specific role, create an output that was handed over to the next in the chain. Job descriptions were put in place so that there was no confusion, leaving behind no room for financial loss, wastage of time and production target slippages. Animators were given work according to their calibre. So even the new artists had a chance to contribute as well as learn from their seniors.

The story idea was always generated by Walter himself, who was like a fountainhead for the studio. Rest of the intellectual assembly line came into action thereafter. Walter insisted that people use fewer words and more drawings. As a story progressed and storyboard was completed, large drawings were put together in the demonstration-cum-music room for Walter to approve or dismiss. Everyone had to sell the project to Walter and, in a way, please him.

The Devil's Advocate

These sessions were very exciting, full of loud deliberations, discussions and even criticism by all those who attended it. While a presentation was being made, Walter used to sit in the middle with a straight face. He rarely divulged what was going on in his mind. He would only jump with joy if he saw something extraordinary; he would sometimes jump out of his chair and often rattle out a few new ideas, sometimes criticizing his own work or earlier suggestions.

When he was bored or disliked something, he would cough a little, raise an eyebrow and thump the table or the arm of the chair again and again, completely immersed in the creative process. These three gestures were a signal that things were not right and were enough to strike fear in the heart of the employee who was pitching an idea to him. He, eventually, started welcoming criticism from other artists in the studio, making it more empowering and democratic; this made the quality of the work as foolproof as possible.

Creating Super Specialization within Specialization

To raise the bar and push for perfection, as he always did, Walter now had artists become specialists in their own core areas. He wanted to assign the right person in the right job. Walter would work on casting these great artists—best in their core competence—as a film director would cast actors for different roles.

He created a database of jokes—a whopping 1.5 million jokes—classified in more than 120 buckets! He had everything in control, an abundance of talent, a lot of resources in every field that was required in cartooning and animation. His aim as usual remained—'Have I created the best or not?' And by now, he was the best.

The Status Games

To avoid another crushing blow of being overworked, Walter, once again, started indulging in outdoor activities and was also involving his staff. He had installed a dummy wooden horse and a cage where staff could practice hitting the ball—much like a driving range for golf.

Now he played polo with the who's who of Hollywood.

'A man should never neglect his family for business.'

—Walter Elias Disney

Baby Boom

Lillian got pregnant again, and this time, Walter was careful to ensure everything went right. Having lived all his life in small tenements, he wanted to now make it grand for his child. He was to build a mansion in the Hollywood Hills for which he set aside a tidy sum of $50,000[18]—a huge amount in the early '30s for a 12-room home.

There was another miscarriage. This was followed by another pregnancy, which saw the birth of his daughter. They named her Diane Marie Disney.

Mickey, his first creation, was doing fine. *The Three Little Pigs* had overshadowed Mickey and he wanted some way to bring back his Mouse to the limelight again. By 1932, the Mickey fan club was doing great, with more than one million members in the US.

The best tribute to Mickey Mouse was when one patient in a hospital, after watching Mickey Mouse, got so overwhelmed that he walked out of the movie theatre without his crutches!

Even Franklin D. Roosevelt, the then US president,

[18]Radloff, Jessica. '30 Stunning Photos From Inside Walt Disney's Home, Plus More Fascinating Disney Secrets!', *Glamour*, 6 October 2014, https://bit.ly/3q4F8ue. Accessed on 14 March 2022.

became an ardent fan of Mickey Mouse. In fact, by now, Mickey Mouse in full colour was ahead of Roosevelt in the popularity list.

Time to Collaborate and Set a New Trend

Roy and Walter were witnessing a revolution by now. Mickey Mouse had become a craze like never before. In fact, they realized that its presence and impact was more outside the theatre than within the four walls of a movie hall. They had to shift the focus to earn more money from Mickey. They wanted merchandise to be manufactured and distributed by the best in the business. They cut a deal for Mickey merchandise with Herman Kamen, who was a hardcore salesman and had risen from grassroots sales force selling on the streets. He promised them that he would augment the business to an extent that they would never be able to imagine, and he did.

This is a lesson for people in business, especially start-ups: they must diversify and that too in their related field. Once you create a business model or a product, try and stay around it so that you don't get trapped in unchartered territory. Walter and Roy saw the potential of proliferating their product and extracting the maximum out of it. The second lesson is to stick to your core competence; in this case, it was to create better and better cartoons, as they were the best in business. Collaborate to sell your stuff with someone who knows marketing and whose core competence is selling.

Now, the brothers had created another full-fledged department of merchandise as an extension of the studio, fully integrated in letter and spirit. They did not want to compromise on the quality and, thus, insisted on getting the best manufacturers who could deliver quality and quantity—exactly what Walter had to do his entire life, making brilliant cartoons one after the other at a breakneck speed. Offers came from big names like General Foods for Mickey Mouse images to be put on their cereal boxes; they were even ready to pay a million dollars for it.

Walter thought that at last they found a good guy like Kamen who was pushing his own boundaries. There were more than 40 contracts related to Mickey Mouse in a short time. Cartier, too, wanted to create a diamond Mickey bracelet. Mickey merchandise was going global. They now had marketing offices in Europe and Australia, with sales touching $35 million in America alone.

The list of products was mindboggling. Soaps, briefcases, boxes, caps, slippers, shoes, mittens, raters, aprons, toffees, umbrellas, raincoats, clocks and chinaware, with more products getting added quickly. Mickey Mouse watches were a hit, so much so the company manufacturing could not cope with the demand. A company making toy trains made Mickey and Minnie hand cars, which sold more than a quarter million pieces in Christmas alone in the year 1934.

Walt Disney Studios was raking in more money from the merchandise than the cartoon itself. It was a case of creating a tail that wagged the mouse!

Mickey brought a smile and could beat your blues and acted as an antidepressant. If the films were great, the impact of merchandise was phenomenal. Walter had yet again proven that he was a trendsetter.

> *'Talent is cheaper than table salt. What separates the talented individual from the successful one is a lot of hard work.'*
>
> —Stephen King

Nothing Can Last Forever

This is another business mantra that has become much more relevant today when we proudly say, 'Change is the only constant.' This was realized in 1935 by Walter, and he knew that they needed another hero, not to replace Mickey Mouse but to add a little more to the already well-burning hearth of the studio; they needed another character that could capture the imagination of the world.

What happened after was purely accidental. Walter heard on the radio a man who mimicked animal voices and called him for an audition. The moment he started singing the song 'Mary had a little lamb' in the voice of a goat, Walter got a duck in his mind. This is how

Donald Duck was born.

They paired Donald Duck and Mickey Mouse together in some sequences. Donald Duck was naughty, malicious and even wicked at times. Troubling others at the drop of the hat was the main attribute of the character.

While Mickey and Minnie were cute, loving and smiling, Donald Duck was self-indulgent, suspicious, rude and hot-headed. Imagine thinking of these multitudes of emotions while keeping an animal or a bird in mind. Imagination then has to be amalgamated with a cartoon flawlessly. How difficult the process must have been, one wonders.

But showing wickedness is probably easier than creating charming sequences with Mickey Mouse. This is why the artists at Disney Studios could roll out Donald Duck cartoons at a faster pace than Mickey's. By now, their processes were set and that might have been a contributing factor to the rapidity in their production.

Disney Studios was on the roll.

Awards Come Tumbling Out

Now, with more than enough dough, name and fame and almost everything a man can hope for, Walter had everything. And he was just 35. From abject poverty, picking up food crumbs from trash cans, losing weight because of malnutrition, having no money to buy a decent suit, harassment at the hands of distributors, colleagues, artists, collaborators, partners, financers and having undergone bouts of anxiety and depressions, he had come a long way. Two people who remained solidly behind him were Lillian, his wife, and Roy, his elder brother.

The topmost pinnacle, according to Maslow's hierarchy of needs, is self-actualization, and with it also comes 'recognition'. No amount of money can help you feel what you do when people in your professional domain recognize you and give you the desired respect. Remember, Walter never craved or clamored for money, he just wanted to be the best in the business.

He became the best in his chosen creative field. No one was near him, in fact, not even within miles. He had already been recognized by the Academy and had earned an Oscar. His drawings were exhibited by the Art Institute of Chicago and he was also bestowed with the membership of The Art Workers' Guild of England, reserved only for literary giants like George Bernard Shaw, Edwin Lutyens and the likes. He was talked about in every leading newspaper and magazine. Celebrities from all walks of life visited Disney Studios and were humbled by his creative prowess.

Yet Walter was grounded and took all the recognition and fame in his stride like a gentleman. He was there to make good cartoons and not money, even when he was being revered by the world.

'Never let your ego get so close to your position that when your position goes, your ego goes with it.'

—Colin Powell

Walter Had a Big Fat Ego

Walter had been rubbed the wrong way too often by too many people and perhaps it got the better of him. At the same time, it is not always easy to handle fame and a cult status. This has happened too often to too many people. Another problem in his case was that he had gone through a constant bad patch in his life right from his early childhood, into his youth, which he could seldom enjoy, and then the upheavals and turbulent times he saw for almost 15 years in his struggle for freedom from financial depravity.

He was indeed a self-made man.

It was clear that it was Walter Elias Disney who was the boss, and people had to accept it. Walter had a big ego and the first sign of its manifestation was when he did not include Roy in the decision-making process while selecting the name for the studio. It was 'Walt Disney Studios' and nothing more or nothing less. In his early days of struggle, he had told Roy that the studio will be called Walt Disney Studios and that is how it was ultimately done.

He had worked on the basic drawings and had done almost everything that could be done with his two hands. So, there was no questioning him on the art and creativity that gave him the name he has till date. He had dirtied his hands while moving up the ladder and that was something he was proud of. He was now there to generate ideas. And that is the most important job of a leader.

By the time he achieved fame, he had stopped working on actual drawings as, by now, he had the best in the business as his team of employees. People at large were not sure as to what exactly he did at the studio. Was he still drawing? Many thought he did, and he wanted people to think that way.

He also wanted every employee of his to be loyal to the name 'Walt Disney' and promote it enthusiastically. A new entrant was told by Walter, 'You are here to do a job and you are here to sell Walt Disney.' He was very honest on this point. As a matter of fact, he said, 'If you want to promote your name, then go somewhere else.' Period.

> *'The architect must be a prophet...a prophet in the true sense of the term...if he can't see at least ten years ahead, don't call him an architect.'*
>
> —Frank Lloyd Wright

8

What Made Walt Disney Walt Disney?

'First, think. Second, dream. Third, believe. And finally, dare.'

—Walter Elias Disney

Walter was undoubtedly the greatest entertainer of the last century and still retains the status. His legacy is unparalleled, and his creations and characters unmatched till today. The quality of his cartoons has never been emulated by anyone. Kids or even adults are still fascinated when they watch a moving Donald Duck or a Mickey Mouse or a Goofy on the screen. Even on TV, they look larger than life and seem to be living creatures and not mere cartoons.

He was revered by his friends, colleagues and loved by his audience. He struggled to survive, went through harrowing experiences, harassment, deceit, double crossing, indignation, insult and handled multiple failures, including bankruptcy, for more than a decade and a half. Here was a man going through such ordeals in his youth when those of his age were enjoying their time. You need to be a man of unusual mettle to go through all this and yet succeed and come out as a winner, finally reaching the pinnacle of success.

Is it possible to analyse what he had in him that others didn't? Can we dissect his mind, his attitude, his stance, his persona, his style of working and, above all, his ability to manage all the failures in his life, taking each blow on his chin bravely and never succumbing to failures?

Apart from being a gifted artist, he had certain other traits that can be emulated by each one of us. These are the qualities that make for a 'success potion', necessary to rise in any business you are a part of. Let us now see what made Walt Disney Walt Disney?

Do What You Love

With this, half the battle is won. Whether having your own business or working for someone else, you need to make an all-out effort to get into something you at least like, if not love. There are options today that were not available to us even two to three decades ago. Thousands of professions allow you the freedom to choose what you love. Here, one thing must be kept in mind: what you love may not be the most economically viable option.

Are you prepared to compromise on money for your love for your work? This is a personal call and that can become a stumbling block. Many people go after a profession that is highly paying and are likely to regret it, as they do not enjoy the work. This leads to a lack of job satisfaction. Today, one works for at least 12 hours a day, which is inclusive of travel time. If half your day goes in sulking, you are not living your life to the fullest. What set Walter apart was his love for his chosen profession and his constant endeavour to get better at it.

Believe in Yourself

Walter was very sure of himself and his craft. You must be self-aware about how well you know what you claim to know. One prerequisite to excel at any work is to be very sure that you know the nuances of what you are entering into. If you don't know how to swim, don't get into a river trying to cross it. It is your ability to swim and not your self-belief that will take you across the river. Therefore, self-belief is a relative term. It is relative to your competence. You can't compete in a math olympiad if you are not brilliant in math. Going only with self-belief without the prerequisite knowledge and skill is like entering a building full of terrorists without a bulletproof jacket.

Once you know that you are good at something, self-confidence will come as a by-product, instilling a feeling of self-belief automatically. This is a practical and foolproof way of proceeding ahead in life.

When you are sure of yourself, you also have to be stubborn at times. And Walter sure was; once he decided to do something, he would not listen to anyone. He was very sure of his judgment and his competence to pull it off.

Take Your Work Seriously

This is a no-brainer. Many people take their work casually and that is a sure recipe for disaster. Along with talent, you need to do your work diligently, giving it your best. How can you excel and improve without being serious about your work? Most of us commit a folly when we tend to become casual and just while away our time.

Never Take Yourself for Granted

You should never be lenient with yourself, no matter what your profession. Many actors fail when they think that they are the best and never take challenges seriously. Similarly, every book an author writes must be written with the same dedication as their previous one. The idea is to never be complacent.

Focus, Focus and More Focus

Many a times, people tend to lose focus and this is not good in the long run. Walter always had rapt attention when a story or a sketch was being discussed. Maintaining such concentration across a 40-year career is difficult, but it is the only way to succeed.

A Perfectionist

To be perfect, be prepared to get into the minutest detail of your work. Why do you think the Germans are proud of their cars or, as a matter of fact, any product? They get into the details while designing and also during production. They do not settle for anything less. The same goes for the Japanese industry and now South Korea too, which are also focusing on precision. Remember that we live in a global world, and if you are less than the best in the business, you will miss the bus. Disney Studios was the best because they always said, 'Can we do better than this?'

That is why Walter's cartoons helped people revisit their childhood days of freedom and happiness, where one could get away from the burdens and realities of adult life.

Don't Make Money Your Goal

Walter worked for a product and never for the money. In

fact, he was always short of money in his bid to make his films better. Money is a by-product; it will automatically come. Your goal should be to make the best you can. Another thing related to this is that if you put a cap to your goals, then your aim is no longer open-ended. For instance, if you say, 'I want to earn ₹20 crore', you will not be able to make more after you earn that much. You must always keep your goals open-ended.

Never Sit Back on Your Past Laurels

I always tell my students that the first job they land from the campus is a mere beginning. Life is a marathon and not a 100-m sprint. You have to prove yourself on the ground in your first job and then keep adding value to your work all the time. Keep sharpening your axe. Therefore, you must never be so happy with your first success that you become complacent. Keep reinventing yourself throughout your career. Walter was very happy with the tumultuous success of Mickey Mouse, but he never sat back on it. He kept on creating new characters constantly.

Commitment and Hard Work

We have all heard the adage 'no pain, no gain'. If you are not prepared to sweat it out, you cannot win a game you are playing. The same principle is applicable when it comes to winning great laurels and success, be it in any field. One must learn from Walter how to stay committed to one's work. He was completely immersed in his craft. Nothing was more important to him than his characters, his studio, his audience, his people and his films.

Be the Best in What You Do

Walter wanted to make the best cartoons in the world and did become the best animator. His was a goal always shrouded in a fog of crippling debt. What is the best and what does it mean to be the best? Is getting an Oscar the guarantee that you are the best? Or does getting a Nobel Prize mean you are the best? Walter had created a position for himself that was indefinable, unreachable and unassailable. And that's what it means to be the best.

Constant Enthusiasm and Energy

One might wonder if Walter ever got tired or fed up of cartoons, the studio and the films he made.

This man had the energy of more than a million horses, as someone in his close circle had said. He could work non-stop for days on an end. Great people have this trait. They always remain motivated because they love their job and they want to be the best at what they are doing. It is as simple as that. To keep yourself on your toes all the time is not easy. But that is what made him Walt Disney.

'If you're going through hell, keep going.'

—Winston Churchill

The Sixth Sense

Now this is largely a gift of God and can't be easily developed, let alone be learnt. It can only be acquired with experience. There is no textbook knowledge available on how to 'acquire' sixth sense. Walter knew what the audience would like and what they wouldn't. He understood the requirement and what the expectations of the people would be, a few years down the line. It was like a gut feeling and a hunch that cannot be explained or put into words.

Lots of marketing gurus from top colleges are not able to sense what will be the trend a few years from now. This is, however, the ultimate quality to become successful. Imagine if you can know what cars will sell after five years and which ones won't, you will be the best car salesman, earning millions. Which coffee will sell over tea or which tea can beat coffee is something very difficult to discern; which movie or genre of books will sell today and what will be the mood of the audience five years from now is extremely difficult to predict. You have to be an astrologer or a magician to do this. However, if you can do it, you are the king.

And Walter was no less.

Understanding Your Market and Tuning Yourself to That

As they say, have your ear to the ground. With an eye on the future, it is extremely important to know the present too. What does your customer want today? And then make efforts to align your product accordingly. For instance, if people have shorter attention spans today, you need to make short clips for advertising and also print books that are not very thick, with shorter and crisper stories. Don't make a product sitting in an ivory tower and say, 'Okay, this is what I feel is the best for you, this is my take on this, and you jolly well buy it.' It will never work.

A Great Salesman

You may have a great product, but you need to pitch it to the person who is going to believe in it and sell it. You write a good book, but you need to convince a good publisher to publish it. Ultimately, what good is a great manuscript if you have no one to publish it? This happens with many authors. J.K. Rowling's first pitch of *Harry Potter* was rejected by 12 publishers. It can be an editorial misjudgment—which often happens—but sometimes an author also falls short in convincing the editorial team.

Walter, a master crafter, was an even bigger master seller. He would go door to door, producer to producer, studio house to studio house and meet everyone, big or small, in the industry who could buy his cartoon films. It was difficult in those days when cartoons were at a nascent stage. He could motivate Technicolor to give him the rights for colour films. He could motivate people to give him money to fund his product. He had that visible passion and the demonstrative commitment that convinced others to buy his ideas.

Without money, which he was always short of, he could have never fulfilled his dream.

Absorbing Technology and Understanding its Potential

A leader in his craft must know the use of technology. He must be abreast of new developments in the field of technology and know which one would be of use to him. For instance, a military general will not know the science behind a missile, but he knows what a cruise missile can do and how to win a war in the future using it. Similarly, a film director should know what kind of modern-day cameras can help with better production.

Today, the entertainment world, especially animation, is all about computer-generated imagery or CGI. You cannot be lagging behind if you are working in the business of cinema.

Walter had that uncanny sense of what he needed and looked out for it wherever he could. That is intellectual creative leadership. Once he decided he wanted sound in his cartoons, he got the best people in business to work on it. He wanted synchronization of sound and moving picture, and pushed the tech guys to create it. He wanted colour and he went after Technicolor. And finally, this pursuit of technological excellence paid rich dividends.

The first-mover advantage is the key in technology. Be the best and be the first.

Resilience

Living in abject poverty and sustaining hardships might create a solid foundation for your career, especially for a start-up. When you leave a cozy job and the precincts of safety, be prepared to rough it out. Today my advice to people founding a start-up is that first learn your craft and how your chosen business works. And for that you need not burn your own savings. Join someone and learn the ropes before you take the plunge. Work in all earnestness so that you learn everything about that business. Save some money and then get into your own venture. Walter was poor and, getting no help from his father, had to start from scratch. Working as a cartoonist for Newspaper Enterprise Association, he made sure to derive maximum experience. He worked harder than others and learnt from his seniors. He sometimes skipped lunch so that he could utilize the time in absorbing every ounce of the craft. He saved a little money and even borrowed some from his brother and close friends.

If you plan properly, you can beat any demanding situation.

Attitude towards Failure

Walter had changed his attitude towards failure and was ready to laugh at himself. He must have lost count of how many times he failed, fumbled and was tricked. He managed to take all of it in his stride. Whenever he had a problem, he would try to shrug it off, seldom showing it on his face. This is not easy.

When *Snow White* was made, this is what happened briefly.

Although *Snow White and The Seven Dwarfs* earned $8 million in its first release[19], the costs of studio expansion and making *Bambi, Dumbo, Fantasia* and *Pinocchio,* added with Walter's ever-present need to push the envelope and amaze the audience, kept the Disney Studios on the financial roller coaster all the way through 1940. By that time, the company had 1,000 employees and a brand new $3-million studio.

Roy called Walter into his office one day to discuss the situation. Roy explained that they owed the bank $4.5 million, and Walter broke out into laughter. Roy demanded to know what was so funny, to which Walter

---

[19]https://bit.ly/3t7DRoc

replied, 'Do you remember when we couldn't borrow a thousand dollars? And now we owe four and a half million... I think that's pretty damn good.'

This was an incredible man who could crack a joke even after being in a 4.5 million-dollar debt![20]

Anyone else would have been happy with what he had achieved. He was, however, fixated with making things better creatively, which left him in a financial crunch most of the time.

Patience

Patience is a virtue without which success will always elude you. Resilience and patience are country cousins. You can't have one without the other. Walter not only had tremendous patience but also demonstrated great stoicism. To be able to continue with this for as long as a couple of decades is something very few can endure. He experienced bad moods, had arguments with colleagues and sometimes could be a little foul-mouthed, but he never gave up in the face of a failure. Even if he had lost everything, he started all over again with the same enthusiasm. This was his greatness.

---

[20]Borucki, Brigitte. 'Walt and Roy Disney: Finding the Balance in Business', Ball State University, Muncie, Indiana, May 2014, https://bit.ly/3J9hEvr. Accessed on 14 March 2022.

Pushing the Envelope

To understand how deep in trouble he was at times, the following should be considered.

It was in 1934, when Walt decided it was time to try for a full-length animated feature. The story was Snow White. He initially estimated that it would cost $500,000 to produce. By the time the two million drawings were combined together into the 83-minute movie, that would balloon to $1,488,422.74. The studio was deeply in debt.[21]

Look at the hard work and commitment, which might come across as absurd to some. However, you don't get to be Walt Disney just like that.

Collaborate, Make Partners, Dreams Alone Won't Do

Yet another great lesson from the legend is, 'You cannot do it alone.'

You need to collaborate with organizations and people who are the best in their craft and line of business. Walter learnt early in life that to sell his cartoons and later his merchandise, he had to tie-up with the best in the business. To showcase his cartoons, he required Hollywood giants like Metro-Goldwyn-Mayer, Warner Brothers, United Artists, Universal Studios and Fox Studios. He bent over backwards to sell his ideas to

---

[21]Ibid.

them. For marketing his merchandise, he got the best person on board and created a studio arm to ensure he could monitor the division, and they made millions.

He got the best musicians, sound engineers, artists and painters as well as story writers. This is a very important lesson for every person in business.

And that is what Americans are good at doing: get the best to create the best and get the best to market that best. This mantra followed by America makes them the largest economy.

The most intriguing part of his personality was that neither did he have that natural charisma, nor did he behave like some snooty Hollywood Czar who arrogated power to themselves by virtue of their position and money. Yet the studio ran as per his wishes, and his sense of what will work and what won't drove the entire creative process. This is one trait every entrepreneur has to have. Be friendly but not familiar; ensure you never let go of the control you hold. Someone may start pushing you into a corner and you may lose everything that you have worked for.

Walter was unpredictable and his moods varied on different days. His employees were eager to gauge his mood each day. One day, he would be very nice and polite and the other day, nasty, where he could be seen snapping at everyone.

As far as creativity goes, he was the ultimate in his understanding of things and he worked with his sixth sense. People at the studio always wanted to understand what Walter wanted and they were ready to do everything they could, out of respect and awe, to satisfy him. It was also difficult to understand what he was thinking. He had a lot to express but found it difficult to explain what his gut feeling was trying to convey.

There came a time when Walter was no longer the lone story generator. People in the story department would make an outline and send it for his approval. He would either give his go-ahead or ask them to work on more possibilities. During story sessions, he seemed as if he was meditating with complete concentration. Sometimes people thought he was not listening and was just staring into oblivion. He was, actually, looking at the sketches put up during the session. One look from him would send a signal that he was about to pounce on you. He was so prepared for every session that his artists were amazed at the way he took his decisions. The day he was quick on the draw meant that he had been to the studio the previous night to go through the sketches to familiarize himself. This is thorough preparedness, and one needs to cultivate this quality in every business.

He was also a great actor and could suddenly transform himself into the character that was being discussed, be it a wolf, a goat or an owl. It came to him very naturally. He would go deeper and deeper into every possible action of a cat or a dog—sniffing, rolling, howling, and so on.

He looked into the smallest of details and could find mistakes that no one else would even notice. He reacted and pointed out things as if he had a microscope in his mind. He would not let even the smallest, most elementary and most insignificant problem pass. It was perfection of the highest order. And is that not evident from every cartoon film of Walt Disney that you have ever watched?

I remember one TV interview of Sanjay Leela Bhansali, an Indian film director who has given many hit Hindi films, where the anchor said, 'There is brilliance in your mind and fingers, you create magic.' Bhansali responded, 'There is no magic, it is all hard work.' And that is what was true for Walter too. You have to be good but being good is not good enough—you got to be perfect by design and hard work.

'It's kind of fun to do the impossible.'

—Walter Elias Disney

A Motivator Par Excellence

Despite his ego, he was a great leader who could motivate his team. He made people feel that they could do the impossible under his guidance. He would raise the bar and charge you up so much that you would volunteer to race up and jump across that high hurdle. Like a perfect rider, he would guide the horse, who might be nervous at first to jump across an obstacle; he would steer, prod, nudge him with his spurs, give a right tug on the reins and ensure that the horse had confidence in the rider while taking the leap.

Most looked up to him in awe and were eager to please him and earn his respect. He had a great gift of making people come up with ideas they did not know they had. They would do something and surpass their own limits of creativity. He was similar to the greatest film directors who could bring out the best in an actor. Greats like Shyam Benegal, Satyajit Ray and Hrishikesh Mukherjee were respected by top actors who gave them the credit for bringing the best out of them. Today we have Shoojit Sircar and Rakesh Omprakash Mehra doing the same.

It was very rare to find Walter not being his enthusiastic self. He was a powerhouse of energy, so much so that he would make one feel equally excited while discussing a story or a visual. It was like generating sympathetic resonance. 'I don't want another film, I want a different, altogether new experience that the audience must be able to feel,' he would say while briefing his artists.

As an entrepreneur, it is your project; the people in your team are only employees. You are committed because you have your skin in the game, while your employees don't have any stake in it and nothing to lose or gain. Can you increase their commitment and hard work to the levels at which you operate? This is where the need of acquired or performed charisma steps in, using which you motivate your employees to work not for the mere pay cheque but work according to your vision and if not more, at least with the same level of commitment as yours. Walter could do that.

The We Factor

In the business of creativity, it is very difficult to get people to bend to your wishes and follow you blindly. This is much easier to achieve in any other business. The biggest ego is of an artist who demands respect and recognition because they bring something new to the world with their creativity. If this was not so, why would people get into the creative field? They could earn their living doing something entirely different.

But an artist is different.

There is an old Indian saying: '*Mazdoor haath se kaam karta hai, kaarigar dimaag se kaam karta hai, aur kalaakaar dil se kaam karta hai* [A labourer works using his hands, a craftsman, his brain, an artist, his heart].'

Therefore, as an entrepreneur you must know how to get work done from an artist whose heart is in his work. Walter did just that.

Another quality of his was that he addressed his employees as his team. He would say, 'We must do this, we can do this, we have achieved this.' Though his was the last word, he always used the word 'we' so that everyone felt they were a part of the project and especially the decision.

> *'Diplomacy is the art of telling people to go to hell in such a way that they ask for directions.'*
>
> —Winston Churchill

Inspiring Awe

You have to be excellent in your work to inspire awe in your subordinates or colleagues. This is the highest you can do to move up the ladder of leadership. However, this is not easy to achieve. You have to be miles ahead in terms of foresight and quicker on the draw from the rest of the pack.

All the qualities and traits put together had helped Walter reach the top of the ladder. People were in awe of him; they looked up to him not because he could bully them but because they respected his creativity. He had what, probably, others did not have—a clear idea of what will sell and what won't. He knew what he and his audience wanted. Some said that as soon as he would enter the discussion room, there would be a hushed silence, as if god of creativity had stepped in. That was the kind of stature he had acquired.

Walt Disney Studios didn't function like any other studio in Hollywood, though there were much larger ones in existence. The entire group working in the studios seemed to be on a mission; there was a zeal within all artists and animators. There was a sense of contributing towards a higher purpose. One of the staffers said, 'It was difficult to understand the aura of this man.'[22] Everyone was out to please him, desperate to draw his attention like a kid and say, 'Hey! I have made something great, please look at it.'

'He had the voice of a prophet and you always had a feeling that he knew what you were going to say and seemed to know things before they happened,' said Joe Grant, an animator at Walt Disney Studios.[23]

There was never a discussion about profits or money. It was craft, craft and craft.

Can an ordinary mortal achieve such legendary heights? Maybe not. Walter Elias Disney, in a way, had emerged as the 'father of cartoonism'. He was a messiah guiding a group of devotees under his leadership, working for a single mission—to be the best.

> *'Success consists of going from failure to failure without loss of enthusiasm.'*
>
> —Winston Churchill

---

[22]Gabler, Neal. *Walt Disney: The Triumph of the American Imagination,* Vintage; reprint edition, 2007.
[23]Ibid.

9

Disney and His Snow White

> *'Creativity involves breaking out of established patterns in order to look at things in a different way.'*
>
> —Edward de Bono

For any entrepreneur worth his salt, one of the most important traits is to keep looking into the future and remain ahead of his competitors. Walter had this inherent quality of looking into the future and actually planning for it years in advance.

Even during the deep recession, his studio was doing well and was earning enough to pay salaries to employees, pay their bills and create the best cartoons even at a hefty cost, without compromising on the quality. He was always restless to keep moving faster than others. He used to look for pointers, which he cleverly observed and kept, stored in a secured corner of his head, to be extracted only when the time was right. He was around 35 and had created great characters like the Three Little Pigs, Mickey Mouse and Donald Duck.

His *Silly Symphony* series got him more than what the competition was getting for their products; it also cost a lot more to keep the Walt Disney benchmark intact. A short film of that genre could cost $30,000 to make and to turn profitable. With all the overheads, marketing and sharing profits, they had to fetch close to $100,000, which was a tall order during the Depression. Yet with his merchandise arm in full swing and other profits from short films in 1934, they made a profit of something to the tune of $600,000.[24] This was a good going considering that America, his prime market, was deep in Depression. He was still looking into the future, expecting the Depression to go away soon.

He had also realized that short films had a short future and they would wane out sooner or later and he had to plan something bigger. He wanted to create a full-length movie and that would cost a bomb. It was not only earning more money that was his consideration for full-length films but his desire to do something which no one had done before. Though short films were earning enough to remain afloat, he wanted the big-ticket stuff. He not only strived to push himself and his team but the medium itself beyond its boundaries

---

[24]Immel, Andrea. 'Merry Christmas, Mickey Mouse! A 1934 Disney Merchandise Promotional Book', *Costen Children's Library,* 13 December 2019, https://bit.ly/3KG9CLc. Accessed on 14 March 2022.

and capabilities. This is like hitting a target at 1,000 yards with a rifle designed for 600-yard range! He always strived for more and also did the impossible.

While he was in Europe, he had seen the audience watch his short films back to back—three of them—cheering and not getting bored or restless. In fact, they remained glued to their seats till the end. This gave him an idea that a full-fledged feature film could also sell. If the film was riveting enough, had a great story to tell and had some very interesting characters, it would make the cut.

In fact, this was a litmus test—witnessing an audience that was totally mesmerized for a considerable time watching cartoons and enjoying it thoroughly. The idea of a feature film had already germinated in his mind a few years ago. This was now a confirmation of the concept that we call 'proving a concept' in management parlance.

Time to Change Track

Once something caught his attention, he had to do it, come what may. He dropped hints about his new venture to the press as well. People also looked at Walter as a force to reckon with in the Hollywood circle, and there were big people suggesting him ideas for making feature films. The ball had started rolling, but where to begin was the question yet to be answered. He was getting inputs from the public and producers that he was getting typecasted in a groove of animals, jungles and trees. He had to move out of this groove—Walter also realized this. He had boxed himself in one groove and needed to break his own shackles now. People suggested working on *Gulliver's Travels* or a remake of *Alice in Wonderland*. But nothing was working out and he could not make up his mind yet. There were offers with people ready to invest, but he was yet to bite the bullet. The time had to be right and, most importantly, the idea had to come from his own mind.

Snow White Is Born

Walter had seen a play, *Snow White,* in his childhood and loved the characters. He decided to make a feature film on this. He also saw his own childhood of struggles in the story, which touched his heart, and loved the idea of seven dwarfs and how he could play with them in the narrative. It had a good storyline and also enough characters to make for a good visual experience.

In as early as 1933, he started working on it, motivating his artists for the project.

A Great Storyteller

Walter was a great storyteller, and people remembered him enacting the entire story in front of them. People would get emotional to the extent that some mentioned about having a lump in their throats. He was a great actor too. When the production started, artists often went back to his recitation whenever they had any doubt. Even for those who had read the story in their childhood, listening to Walter was a unique experience. This is what a showman is supposed to do.

When he explained this to his animators, they were dumbstruck and wanted to do just what he enacted. By the end of 1934, he had his team ready and motivated for the job. He could explain it to an artist and a layman, too, with equal ease. And that meant he knew exactly what he wanted.

> *'If you can't explain it to a six-year-old, you don't understand it yourself.'*
>
> —Albert Einstein

Music and Songs

Now was the time for action, and music was a very important part of the entire project. Great directors get involved in everything. Though, technically, he was not directing the film, it was his concept, and he wanted it just right. He tasked Frank Edwin Churchill to head the music composition and the entire track for the film. He wrote most of the lyrics of the songs in *Snow White and the Seven Dwarfs*, including 'Heigh-Ho', 'Whistle While You Work' and 'Some Day My Prince Will Come'.

Investment and Production

Walter wanted a good distributor and financer as Walt Disney Studios did not have so much money to put in. Around 500 employees were deputed for this project and he was hiring more talent, which he thought was a must. It was finally produced and ready for launch in February 1937 (it took over four years for it to take-off), and it became a benchmark in the animation industry. The film was backed and distributed by RKO Radio Pictures.

The production cost was $1.49[25] million and the box office collection was $418 million![26]

The movie had a runtime of 83 minutes. The entire movie was made by artists with hand-drawn pictures; a total of estimated 400,000 pictures were created, out of which around 120,000 were selected and used for the 83-minute film that required 24 frames per second. What a colossal effort! Walter was personally looking into every aspect of the film. Four thousand colours were used in the palette by the artists to make it as mesmerizingly real as possible. It all worked!

This was an all-time record as a commercial as

---

[25]Barrier, Michael. *Hollywood Cartoons: American Animation in Its Golden Age*. Oxford University Press, New York, 1999.

[26]Wilhelm, Henry Gilmer and Carol Brower. *The Permanence and Care of Color Photographs: Traditional and Digital Color Prints, Color Negatives, Slides, and Motion Pictures.* Grinnell, Iowa, 1993.

well as creative success in the history of cinema, contributing to the making of the great Walt Disney.

'It takes 20 years to make an overnight success.'

—Eddie Cantor

Lessons from Walt Disney

1. Identify your passion and pursue it. Be sure to know that it is your passion and not a fad.
2. Work towards your passion.
3. The four Ps of success are passion, potential, purpose and perseverance.
4. Take whatever experience you can get. Learn more than earn.
5. Don't worry about the specific goal, let the fog remain.
6. Don't look at fixing a monetary target; be the best cartoonist, the best designer, the best engineer.
7. Persevere with the work you love.
8. Be proud of and happy with small achievements.
9. Praise and recognition of your work is more important than money if you want to make it big.
10. Use the first-mover advantage—get ahead of others.
11. Always pay back your debts even after you go bankrupt.
12. Never lose heart and remain hopeful.
13. Be where the action is.
14. Build a reputation of being honest and truthful. Build transparency and return what you owe.

15. Take criticism as constructive suggestions if you want to improve.
16. Be the master of your craft. Do everything with your own hands initially so that you know every aspect of your work. Thereafter, no one can trick you or hold you to ransom.
17. You must learn from your coworkers.
18. It is difficult to get good people to work for you when you are new in the business and even more difficult to retain them.
19. Initially, don't draw a big fat salary so as not to drain the system.
20. One cannot completely trust anyone—not even your own people or even friends at work.
21. Never sign before taking sound advice from someone who knows the commercial math.
22. It is not quality of work alone but the benchmark of expectation that we are the best that should be the mantra for success.
23. In marketing, if you want to succeed, you must do carpet bombing. All guns blazing simultaneously—that is how a cult is created.
24. Keep your cards close to the chest to avoid any espionage or ambush.
25. The best of ideas will not see the light of the day if there is no support from good investors.
26. People in business, especially start-ups, must diversify and that too in their own related field. Once you create a business model or a product, try

and stay around it so that you don't get trapped in unchartered territory.

27. Stick to your core competence.
28. Collaborate to sell your stuff with someone who knows marketing and whose core competence is selling.
29. Be friendly but not familiar and also ensure you never let go of the control or else you might regret it one day. Someone may start pushing you into a corner and you may lose everything that you have ever worked for.
30. As an entrepreneur, it is your project and the rest of them are employees. You are committed because you have your skin in it, while the employees don't have any stake in it and have nothing to lose or gain. Can you get their commitment and hard work to the levels at which you operate? This is the 'acquired or performed charisma' that you need to create in front of your people so that they don't work for the pay but according to your vision, and if not more, at least with the same level of commitment as yours.

14·6·62